Certified Ethical Hacker v11

Exam Cram Notes

First Edition

Chapter 01: Introduction to Ethical Hacking

Information Security Overview

System security refers to the methods and procedures for preventing unauthorized access, disclosure, use, or modification of data and information systems. Information security ensures that data is kept confidential, secure, and accessible. An organization's confidential information and data will not be secure if it lacks security policies and suitable security standards, placing the organization in danger. Security policies and well-defined procedures can help secure an organization's assets from unauthorized access and disclosure.

It is necessary to understand some essential cyber security terminology. These terminologies will help understanding information security concepts.

- Hack Value
- Zero-Day Attack
- Vulnerability
- Daisy Chaining
- Exploit
- Doxing
- Payload

Data Breaches

eBay Data Breach

The data breach at eBay is a well-known example of the importance of corporate information and network security. eBay is a well-known online auction site utilized by millions of people worldwide.

Google Play Hack

Ibrahim Balic, a Turkish hacker, hacked Google Play twice. He claimed responsibility for the Google Play hack and admitted to being behind Apple's Developer site attack. He discovered a weakness in the Android Operating System while testing vulnerabilities in Google's Developer Console. He double-checked the bug to ensure that it was legitimate and then used the results of his vulnerability testing to create an Android app to exploit the flaw. Users could not download applications, while developers could not post their applications after their console broke.

The Home Depot Data Breach

In response to the attack, Home Depot took corrective action. They began accepting EMV Chip and Pin cards. To prevent duplication of the magnetic stripe, these Chip and Pin payment cards feature a security chip integrated into them. Fraudulent transactions are prevented using EMV cards.

Elements of Information Security

Confidentiality

Only authorized individuals have access to and can operate with our infrastructure's digital resources.

Integrity

According to the NIST, "guarding against improper information alteration or deletion, including insuring information non-repudiation and authenticity." Unauthorized people should never be able to alter or misrepresent our sensitive or confidential data. According to data integrity, only authorized parties are allowed to update data.

Availability

Availability refers to the capacity to access and use information applied to systems and data in a timely and reliable manner. If authorized workers are unable to access data as a result of a general network failure or a Denial-of-Service (DOS) attack, it is regarded a critical problem from a business standpoint, since it may result in the loss of income or important documents.

Authenticity

Authenticity assures that some information is appropriate and that it was begun by a legitimate user who claims to be the source of that information.

Authenticity can be established through the authentication procedure.

Non-Repudiation

One of the cornerstones of Information Assurance (IA) is non-repudiation. It uses several techniques, such as digital signatures and encryption, to ensure the transmission and reception of information between the sender and receiver. Non-repudiation is the assurance of communication and its authenticity, such that the sender cannot refute the message sent.

The Security, Functionality, and Usability Triangle

The level of security in a system is a measure of the system's strength in terms of security, functionality, and usability. The Security, Functionality, and Usability triangle is made up of these three elements. Consider the ball's position in this triangle: all three components are stronger if the ball is in the center. Suppose the ball is closer to Security, on the other hand. In that case, it suggests the system uses more resources for Security, and its Function and Usability need to be addressed. A secure system must deliver robust security and comprehensive services, functionality, and usability to the user.

Threats and Attack Vectors

Motives, Methods, and Vulnerabilities

An attacker strikes the target system with three attack vectors in mind to breach information security: motive or objective, method, and vulnerability. These three elements are the main building blocks of an attack.

- **Motive or Objective:** The reason an attacker focuses on a particular system
- **Method:** The technique or process used by an attacker to gain access to a target system
- **Vulnerability:** These help the attacker in fulfilling his intentions

Top Information Security Attack Vectors

Cloud Computing Threats

Today, cloud computing is a popular trend. Its broad use has made it vulnerable to several security risks. The majority of the hazards are comparable to those that traditionally hosted settings have to deal with. Cloud computing must be secured to protect sensitive and secret information.

Advanced Persistent Threats

The technique of stealing information through a continuous method is known as an Advanced Persistent Threat (APT). A persistent advanced threat usually targets private organizations or political agendas.

Viruses and Worms

Malicious software is referred to as a virus in network and information security. This dangerous malware spreads by affixing itself to other files. It helps it transfer to other systems by attaching itself to other files. Some viruses require user involvement to activate, infect, and commence malicious actions on the resident system.

Worms, unlike viruses, are capable of self-replication. Worms can swiftly spread on a resident system because of this ability.

Mobile Threats

Emerging mobile phone technology, particularly smartphones, has increased the target of mobile device attacks. As smartphones became more widely used worldwide, attackers focused on stealing commercial and personal data via mobile devices.

Insider Threat

An insider can also misuse a system within a corporate network. Users are termed "Insider" and have different privileges and authorization power to access and grant the network resources.

Botnets

Botnets are a collection of bots connected via the internet to carry out a distributed task continually. They're renowned as the internet's workhorses. These botnets use the internet to do repetitive tasks (Robot) (Network). Botnets are most commonly found in Internet Relay Chat rooms. Botnets of this type are both legal and beneficial.

Threat Categories

Information Security Threats can be categorized as follows:

- Network Level Threats
- Host Level Threats
- Application Level Threats

Operating System Attacks

In operating system attacks, vulnerable OS versions are mostly targeted. Sometimes, a newer update of an OS also brings a zero-day. This is a continuous cycle of finding bugs and vulnerabilities in the source code and patching it.

Information Warfare

Information warfare is a concept of warfare over control of information. The term "Information Warfare" or "Info War" describes the use of Information and Communication Technology (ICT) to get a competitive advantage over an opponent or rival. Information warfare is classified into two types:

Defensive Information Warfare

"Defensive Information Warfare" refers to all defensive actions taken to protect oneself from attacks executed to steal information and information-based processes.

Offensive Information Warfare

Offensive warfare is an aggressive operation taken against a rival proactively rather than waiting for the attackers to attack. Accessing their territory to occupy it rather than lose it is the fundamental concept of offensive warfare.

Cyber Kill Chain Concepts

Lockheed Martin developed the Cyber Kill Chain framework. It is an intelligence-driven defense model for identifying, detecting, and preventing cyber intrusion activity by understanding the adversary tactics and techniques during the complete intrusion cycle. This framework helps to identify and enhance the visibility into a cyber-attack. It also helps blue teams in understanding the tactics of APT's. There are seven steps of the Cyber Kill Chain.

1. Reconnaissance
2. Weaponization
3. Delivery
4. Exploitation
5. Installation
6. Command and Control
7. Actions on Objectives

Hacking Concepts

The term hacking in information security refers to exploiting vulnerabilities in a system and compromising the security to gain unauthorized command and control of the system. The purpose of hacking may include altering a system's resources or disrupting features and services to achieve other goals. Hacking can also be used to steal confidential information for any use, such as sending it to competitors, regulatory bodies, or publicizing it.

Hacker

A Hacker is a person capable of stealing information such as business data, personal data, financial information, credit card information, username, and password from a system she or he has no authorized access to. An attacker gains access by taking unauthorized control over that system using different techniques and tools.

Hacking Phases

The following are the five phases of hacking:

1. Reconnaissance
2. Scanning
3. Gaining Access
4. Maintaining Access
5. Clearing Tracks

Ethical Hacking Concepts

Ethical hacking and penetration testing are common terms and have been popular in information security environments for a long time. The increase in cybercrimes and hacking has created a great challenge for security experts, analysts, and regulations over the last decade. The virtual war between hackers and security professionals has become very common.

Why Ethical Hacking is Necessary

The rising number of malicious activities and cybercrimes and the appearance of different advanced attacks have created the need for ethical hacking. An ethical hacker penetrates the security of systems and networks to determine their security level and advises organizations to take precautions and remediation actions against aggressive attacks. These aggressive and advanced attacks include:

- Denial-of-Services Attacks
- Manipulation of Data
- Identity Theft
- Vandalism
- Credit Card Theft

- Piracy
- Theft of Services

Phases of Ethical Hacking

Ethical Hacking is the combination of the following phases:

- Footprinting and Reconnaissance
- Scanning
- Enumeration
- System Hacking
- Escalation of Privileges
- Covering Tracks

Skills of an Ethical Hacker

An expert ethical hacker has a set of technical and non-technical skills, as outlined below:

Technical Skills

1. Ethical Hackers have in-depth knowledge of almost all Operating Systems, including all popular, widely-used OSes such as Windows, Linux, Unix, and Macintosh.
2. Ethical hackers are skilled at networking, basic and detailed concepts, technologies, and exploring hardware and software capabilities.
3. Ethical hackers have a strong command over security areas, information security-related issues, and technical domains.
4. They must have detailed knowledge of all older, advanced and sophisticated attacks.

Non-Technical Skills

1. Learning ability
2. Problem-solving skills
3. Communication skills
4. Committed to security policies
5. Awareness of laws, standards, and regulations

Information Security Controls

Information Security Controls are safeguards or procedures put in place to reduce the danger of a cyber attack and detect and neutralize information security threats to a business. Data exfiltration, data breaches, and illegal access are all possible hazards. These information security controls to aid in the protection of the CIA's information security triad.

Information Assurance (IA)

Information Assurance, in short, IA, depends upon Integrity, Availability, Confidentiality, and Authenticity. Combining these components guarantees information and information systems and their protection during usage, storage, and communication.

Information Security Policies

Information Security Policies are the fundamental and most dependent component of any information security infrastructure. Fundamental security requirements, conditions, and rules are configured to be enforced in an information security policy to secure the organization's resources. These policies cover the outlines of management, administration, and security requirements within an information security architecture.

The basic goals and objectives of Information Security Policies are:

- Cover security requirements and conditions of the organization
- Protect the organization's resources
- Eliminate legal liabilities
- Minimize the wastage of resources
- Prevent unauthorized access/modification etc.
- Minimize risks
- Information Assurance

Categories of Security Policies

The different categories of security policies are as follows:

1. Promiscuous Policy
2. Permissive Policy
3. Prudent Policy
4. Paranoid Policy

Information Security Management Program

Information Security Management programs are specifically developed to focus on lowering information security risks and vulnerabilities. This is done to prepare organizations and users to work in less vulnerable environments.

Enterprise Information Security Architecture (EISA)

Enterprise Information Security Architecture is a set of requirements and processes for establishing, examining, and monitoring an information system's structure and behavior.

Threat Modeling
Threat modeling is a method or strategy for discovering, diagnosing, and assessing a system's or application's risks and vulnerabilities. It is a threat assessment method that focuses on examining systems and applications while keeping security objectives in mind.

Network Security Zoning
Managing and deploying an organization's architecture in different security zones is called Network Security Zoning. These security zones are a set of network devices with a specific security level.

Physical Security
When it comes to safeguarding anything, physical security is always the priority. It is also regarded as the first layer of protection in the field of information security.

Incident Management
Incident Response Management is the procedure and method of handling any incident that occurs. This incident may be a violation of any condition, policy, etc. Similarly, in information security, incident responses are the remediation actions or steps taken to respond to an incident to make the system stable, secure, and functional again. The duties and responsibilities of penetration testers, users, or company employees are defined by incident response management.

Incident Management Process
Incident Response Management processes include:

1. Preparation for Incident Response
2. Detection and Analysis of Incident Response
3. Classification of an incident and its prioritization
4. Notification and Announcements
5. Containment
6. Forensic Investigation of an Incident
7. Eradication and Recovery
8. Post-Incident Activities

Incident Response Team
An Incident Response team is made up of people who are well-versed in dealing with incidents. This response team consists of highly trained professionals in gathering information and securing any evidence of an assault gathered from the incident system.

Vulnerability Assessment
Vulnerability assessment is the process of investigating, identifying, and analyzing a system's or application's ability to withstand any threat, including security procedures functioning on the system. Using vulnerability assessment, you can detect weaknesses in a system, prioritize vulnerabilities, and evaluate any additional security layer's need for and effectiveness.

Types of Vulnerability Assessment
Following are the types of vulnerability assessment:

1. Active Assessment
2. Passive Assessment
3. Host-based Assessment
4. Internal Assessment
5. External Assessment
6. Network Assessment
7. Wireless Network Assessment
8. Application Assessment Network

Penetration Testing
Penetration Testing is the process of hacking a system, with permission from the owner of that system, to evaluate security, Hack Value, Target of Evaluation (TOE), attacks, exploits, zero-day vulnerability, and other components such as threats vulnerabilities, and daisy-chaining. In the environment of Ethical Hacking, a pentester is an individual authorized by an owner to hack into a system to perform penetration testing.

Types of Penetration Testing
- Black Box
- Gray Box
- White Box

Phases of Penetration Testing
Penetration Testing is a three-phase process:

1. Pre-Attack Phase
2. Attack Phase
3. Post-Attack Phase

Information Security Laws and Standards

Law is a rule created and enacted by the judicial system of a country. Similarly, International laws are created by mutual understandings and applicable across the globe. Any violation of these laws can be prosecuted in the national or international court. Cyber laws are focused on information and cybersecurity. These laws specify adoptions, restrictions, mandatory compliance, and other legal aspects.

Payment Card Industry Data Security Standard (PCI-DSS)

The PCI Security Standards Council produced the Payment Card Industry Data Security Standard (PCI-DSS), a global information security standard. It was intended to help businesses develop, improve, and evaluate cardholder information and payment account security standards.

ISO/IEC 27001:2013

The International Organization for Standardization (ISO) and International Electro-Technical Commission (IEC) globally develop and maintain their standards. ISO/IEC 2700 1:20 13 standard ensures the implementation, maintenance, and improvement of an information security management system.

Health Insurance Portability and Accountability Act (HIPAA)

It establishes the national standards and safeguards that must be implemented to secure electronically protected health information. The HIPAA defines general rules for risk analysis and management of E-PHI.

Industry-Standard Framework and Reference Architecture

A conceptual model that explains the function and structure of an IT system in any organization is known as an industry-standard framework and reference architecture.

- Regulatory
- Non-Regulatory
- National vs. International
- Industry-Specific Framework
- Benchmarks/Secure Configuration Guides
- Platform-Specific Guide

Chapter 02: Footprinting and Reconnaissance

Footprinting Concepts

Footprinting is the initial stage in ethical hacking. Footprinting entails acquiring as much information as possible about the target and target network. The data gathered aids in the identification of various entry points into the target network.

Pseudonymous Footprinting

The collecting of information about a target through online sources is known as pseudonymous footprinting. Information about a target is released on the internet by someone other than the target in pseudonymous footprinting. This type of information is shared without real credentials to avoid being traced to the actual source of information. The author may be a corporate or government figure who isn't allowed to publish under his or her own name.

Internet Footprinting

Footprinting and reconnaissance methods for acquiring information via the internet are included in Internet Footprinting. The Google hacking database, Google Advanced Search, and a few other search engines are popular tools for internet footprinting.

Objectives of Footprinting

The footprinting objectives are:

1. To know security posture
2. To reduce the focus area
3. To identify vulnerabilities
4. To draw a network map

Footprinting Methodology

The internet, social media, official websites, and a few other similar sources have made it easy for hackers to get information about whomever they want. It does not require much effort to gather information from these sources. The information available on public sources may not be sensitive, but it might be enough to fulfill the hacker's requirements. Hackers often use the following platforms for gathering information:

- Search Engines
- Advanced Google Hacking Techniques
- Social Networking Sites
- Websites
- Email
- Competitive Intelligence
- WHOIS
- DNS
- Network
- Social Engineering

Footprinting through Search Engines

Footprinting using search engines is the most basic and responsive technique. Search engines scavenge the internet for material on any topic. You can search for whatever you want using a web browser and a search engine like Google or Bing. The search engine returns results that include all available information on the internet.

Footprinting through Web Services

During collecting information, an attacker also collects information about an organization's official website, including its public and restricted URLs. The official website's URL can simply be obtained through search engines, as previously explained. However, to find the restricted URL of an organization's website, the attacker will have to use different services to fetch information from websites.

Location Information

After collecting the necessary information through search engines and different services like Netcraft and Shodan. Information like the physical location of the headquarters, what surrounds it, the location of branch offices, and other related information can be collected from online location and map services.

Online People Search Services

Apart from websites, now you can search about people using their contact numbers or residential addresses. Most of these sites are maintained and accessible regionally. These online services are available for looking up people's phone numbers and addresses.

Job Sites

On Job Sites, organizations that offer job vacancies provide their organization's information, portfolio, and job post. This information includes the company's location, industry information, contact information, the number of employees, job requirements, and hardware and software information. Similarly, personal information can be collected from a targeted individual by posting a fake job vacancy on such sites.

Monitoring a Target Using Alerts

Google, Yahoo, and other search engines offer alert services for content monitoring, updated notification for webpages, news, blogs and articles, scientific researches, and intelligence.

Groups, Forums, and Blogs

Groups, forums, blogs, and communities can be great sources of sensitive information. Joining these platforms using a fake ID and accessing the target organization's group is not difficult for anyone these days. Any official and non-official group can become a source for the leakage of sensitive information.

Footprinting Using Advanced Google Hacking Techniques

- Google Advanced Search Operators
- Google Hacking Database (GHDB)

Website Footprinting

Monitoring and researching the target organization's official website for information such as the software being used, its versions, Operating Systems, sub-directories, database, scripting information, and other facts are known as website footprinting.

Email Footprinting

Email plays an essential role in running an organization's business. Email is one of the most popular, widely used, professional methods of communication and is used by every organization for communicating with partners, employees, competitors, contractors, and other people involved in the organization's daily business. The content or the body of an email is extremely valuable to attackers.

Competitive Intelligence

Competitive Intelligence is an approach to collecting information and analyzing and gathering competitors' statistics. Competitive Intelligence is non-interfering as it is the process of collecting information through different resources. Some primary sources of competitive intelligence are:

- Official Websites
- Job Advertisements
- Press Releases
- Annual Reports
- Product Catalogs
- Analysis Reports
- Regulatory Reports
- Agents, Distributors, and Suppliers

Monitoring Website Traffic

Some website monitoring tools are being widely used by developers, attackers, and penetration testers to check the statistics of websites. These tools include Web-Stat and Alexa as popular tools for monitoring website traffic.

WHOIS Footprinting

WHOIS Lookup

"WHOIS" searches its database for information on domain names and ownership, as well as IP addresses, Netblock data, Domain Name Servers, and other details. The WHOIS database is maintained by Regional Internet Registries (RIR). The WHOIS Lookup tool can be used to determine who owns the domain name in question.

DNS Footprinting

For identifying a host within a targeted network, DNS lookup information is useful. DNS lookup can be done with a variety of tools available on the internet.

Network Footprinting

One of the most important types of footprinting is Network Footprinting. Fortunately, several tools are available that can be used for network footprinting to gain information about the target network. An information seeker can use these technologies to construct a map of the targeted network and extract data such as:

- Network address ranges
- Hostnames

- Exposed hosts
- OS and application version information
- The patch state of the host and the applications
- The structure of the applications and back-end servers

Social Engineering

The art of obtaining sensitive information from people is known as social engineering. Social Engineers manipulate human psychology to persuade others to share sensitive information. In Information Security, footprinting through social engineering is done for gathering information such as:

- Credit card information
- Usernames and passwords
- Security devices and technology information
- Operating System information
- Software information
- Network information
- IP address and name server's information

Eavesdropping

Eavesdropping is a type of Social Engineering footprinting in which the social engineer acquires information by listening in on conversations without being detected. Listening, reading, and accessing any source of information without being discovered are all examples of this.

Phishing

In the process of Phishing, emails sent to a targeted group contain messages that look legitimate. The recipient clicks on the URL provided in the email, believing it to be genuine. When the reader hits the link, they are taken to a false website that appears official. For example, the recipient may be redirected to a fake bank web page asking for sensitive information. Similarly, clicking on the link may download a malicious script onto the recipient's system to fetch information.

Shoulder Surfing

Shoulder Surfing is a technique that involves standing behind a target as he is dealing with sensitive material and collecting information. Passwords, account numbers, and other sensitive information can be collected using this technique, depending on the target's carelessness.

Dumpster Diving

Dumpster Diving is the act of searching through the trash for hidden treasure. This method is old, but it still works. It entails searching through the target's trash, such as the printer trash, user desk trash, and company trash, for phone bills, contact information, financial information, source codes, and other useful information.

Countermeasures of Footprinting

Footprinting countermeasures include the following:

- An organization's employees' access to social networking sites from the corporate network must be restricted
- Devices and servers should be configured to avoid data leakage
- Education, training, and awareness regarding footprinting, its impact, methodologies, and countermeasures should be provided to employees
- Revealing sensitive information in annual reports, press releases, etc. should be avoided
- Prevent search engines from caching web pages

Chapter 03: Scanning Networks

Introduction

Network Scanning obtains network information about hosts, ports, etc., and running services by scanning the networks and their ports. The main Objective of Network Scanning is:

- To identify live hosts on a network
- To identify open and closed ports
- To identify Operating System information
- To identify services running on a network
- To identify processes running on a network
- To identify the presence of security devices like firewalls
- To identify system architecture
- To identify running services
- To identify vulnerabilities

An Overview of Network Scanning

The Scanning Network phase includes probing the target network to get information. When a user probes another user, the received reply can reveal very useful information. In-depth identification of networks, ports, and running services helps create a network architecture, and the attacker gets a clearer picture of the target.

TCP Communication

There are two types of Internet Protocol (IP) traffic. The two protocols are TCP (Transmission Control Protocol) and UDP (Uniform Datagram Protocol) (User Datagram Protocol). TCP (Transmission Control Protocol) is a connection-oriented protocol. Bidirectional communication occurs after the successful creation of a link.

ICMP Scanning

ICMP Scanning is a method of verifying if a host is alive by sending it ICMP Echo requests. An ICMP Echo reply packet received from a host confirms the host's existence. Ping Scanning is a useful tool for determining whether a host is alive and whether ICMP packets are routed past firewalls and the TTL value.

Ping Sweep

Ping Sweep determines live hosts on a large scale. Ping Sweep is a method of sending ICMP echo request packets to a range of IP addresses instead of sending requests one by one and observing the response.

Ports & Services Discovery

SSDP Scanning

Simple Service Discovery Protocol (SSDP) is a protocol used for discovering network services without the assistance of server-based configuration like Dynamic Host Configuration Protocol (DHCP), Domain Name System (DNS), and static network host configuration. SSDP can discover Plug and Play devices with UPnP (Universal Plug and Play). SSDP protocol is compatible with IPv4 and IPv6.

Netscan

NetScan Tools Pro is an application that collects information, performs network troubleshooting, monitoring, discovery, and diagnostics using its integrated tools designed for the Windows-based Operating System, which offers a focused examination of IPv4, IPv6, domain names, email, and URL using automatic and manual options.

Scanning Techniques

Scanning techniques include UDP and TCP scanning. The following figure shows the classification of scanning techniques:

- TCP Connect / Full Open Scan
- Stealth Scan (Half-Open Scan)
- Inverse TCP Flag Scanning
- Xmas Scan
- FIN Scan
- NULL Scan
- ACK Flag Probe Scanning
- IDLE/IPID Header Scan
- UDP Scanning

Scanning Beyond IDS

Attackers employ fragmentation to get around security devices like firewalls, intrusion detection systems, and intrusion prevention systems. Splitting the payload into smaller packets is the most widely used and widely used approach. To investigate and detect the assault, the IDS must reconstruct the incoming packet stream. These tiny packets are changed to make packet reassembly and detection more difficult.

OS Fingerprinting & Banner Grabbing

OS Fingerprinting is a technique used to identify the information of an Operating System running on a target machine. By gathering information about the Operating System being run, an attacker can determine the vulnerabilities and possible bugs that the OS may possess. The two types of OS Fingerprinting are as follows:

1. Active OS Fingerprinting
2. Passive OS Fingerprinting

Draw Network Diagrams

To obtain access to a network, you will need a thorough understanding of its design and precise information. An attacker can better grasp the network diagram if they have valuable network information such as security zones, security devices, routing devices, and the number of hosts. A network diagram defines a logical and physical path to the proper target within a network once designed.

Network Discovery Tool

OpManager is a sophisticated network monitoring tool that can handle faults on WAN lines, routers, switches, VoIP, and servers. It's also capable of managing performance. Network View is a network discovery tool with a lot of features. It can identify routes, TCP/IP nodes, ports, and other network protocols via DNS. Some popular tools are listed below:

1. Network Topology Mapper
2. OpManager
3. Network View
4. LANState Pro

Proxy Servers

To provide anonymity, proxy servers anonymize online traffic. A proxy server works as a middleman between a user and the other publicly available servers when a user seeks access to any resource. The proxy server receives the user's request first. These requests can take the shape of a web page request, a file download request, a connection request to another server, and so on.

Proxy Chaining

Proxy Chaining is a method of utilizing numerous proxy servers. The traffic is forwarded to the next proxy server by one proxy server. This method is not suitable for use in production settings, nor is it a long-term solution.

Proxy Tool

Various proxy tools are available, and you may also look for a proxy server online and manually configure it in your web browser. There are several proxy tools available, including:

- Proxy Switcher
- Proxy Workbench
- TOR
- CyberGhost

Introduction to Anonymizers

Anonymizer is a tool that completely hides or removes identity-related information to make activities untraceable. The basic purposes of using anonymizers are to minimize risk, identify and prevent information theft, bypass restrictions and censorship, and carry out untraceable activity on the internet.

Chapter 04: Enumeration

Enumeration Concepts

Enumeration

An attacker establishes active connections with the target system during the Enumeration phase. Direct requests are generated to obtain more information through this active connection. This information aids in the identification of the system's weak points. Once an attacker has identified attack sites, he or she can use the information gathered to obtain unauthorized access to the assets.

The information enumerated in this phase is:

- Routing Information
- SNMP Information
- DNS Information
- Machine Name
- User Information
- Group Information
- Application and Banners
- Network Sharing Information
- Network Resources

Techniques for Enumeration

- Enumeration Using an Email ID
- Enumeration Using Default Password
- Enumeration using SNMP
- Brute Force Attack on Active Directory
- Enumeration through DNS Zone Transfer

NetBIOS Enumeration

NetBIOS stands for Network Basic Input/Output System. It is a program that allows communication between different applications running on different systems within a local area network. NetBIOS uses a unique 16-ASCII character string to identify the network devices over TCP/IP. The initial 15 characters are for identifying the device; the 16th character is to identify the service. NetBIOS service uses TCP port 139. NetBIOS over TCP (NetBT) uses the following TCP and UDP ports:

- UDP port 137 (name services)
- UDP port 138 (datagram services)
- TCP port 139 (session services)

NetBIOS Enumeration Tool

The nbtstat command is a handy tool for viewing statistics about NetBIOS over TCP/IP. It is also used to show information like NetBIOS name tables, name cache, and other things.

SMB Enumeration

Server Message Block (SMB) protocol in Windows is used for resource sharing. Resources like printing, file sharing, or others can be hosted and retrievable via SMB protocol. An authorized user or application can access resources within a network. It runs over port 139 or 445. Windows natively support SMB protocol; however, for Linux, a samba server is needed to be installed because Linux does not natively support SMB protocol.

SMB Enumeration Tools

Following are the list of interesting tools used for SMB enumeration:

- Enum4Linux
- SMBClient
- SMBMap
- NSE Scripts

SNMP Enumeration

Simple Network Management Protocol (SNMP) enumeration is a technique in which information regarding user accounts and devices is targeted using the most widely used network management protocol, SNMP. SNMP requires a community string to authenticate the management station.

SNMP Enumeration Tool

- OpUtils
- SolarWinds Engineer's Toolset

LDAP Enumeration

The Lightweight Directory Access Protocol LDAP is an open standard internet protocol. LDAP is used for accessing and maintaining distributed directory information services in a hierarchical and logical structure. A directory service plays an important role by allowing user, system, network, service information, etc., to be shared throughout the network. LDAP provides a central place to store usernames and passwords.

NTP Enumeration

Network Time Protocol (NTP)

Network Time Protocol (NTP) is a protocol for synchronizing clocks across hosts and network devices in a network. NTP is a critical protocol because clock settings are used by directory services, network devices, and hosts to log in and keep track of events. NTP aids in the correlation of events by the time Syslog servers receive system logs. NTP communicates through UDP port 123 and is based on Coordinated Universal Time (UTC).

NTP Authentication

NTP version 3 (NTPv3) and advanced versions support a cryptographic authentication technique between NTP peers. This authentication can be used to mitigate an attack.

NFS Enumeration

NFS allows hosts running different operating systems, such as Windows, Linux, or Unix, to mount file systems via a network. Because the files are mounted locally, mounting a file system makes it easier to access them. This allows system administrators to consolidate resources on the network's centralized servers. NFS protocol comprises NFS Server and Client functionalities in Windows Server.

SMTP Enumeration

Simple Mail Transfer Protocol (SMTP)

Using the Simple Mail Transfer Protocol, SMTP Enumeration is another approach to extract information about the target (SMTP). Over internet port 25, the SMTP Protocol guarantees email connectivity between email servers and recipients. SMTP is a TCP/IP protocol that is commonly used by most email servers and is presently described in RFC 821.

SMTP Enumeration Tool

- NetScan Tool Pro
- SMTP-user-enum
- Telnet

DNS Zone Transfer Enumeration

An attacker discovers the target's TCP port 53 during the enumeration process via DNS Zone transfer, like TCP port 53 is used by DNS, and Zone transfer utilizes this port by default. You can use port scanning techniques to determine whether or not a port is open.

DNS Zone Transfer

DNS Zone Transfer is a DNS function that DNS does. During the Zone transfer process, DNS sends a copy of the database records to another DNS server because many DNS servers can reply to queries, the DNS Zone transfer mechanism aids in query resolution.

Enumeration Countermeasures

Countermeasures for preventing enumeration are as follows:

1. Use advanced security techniques.
2. Install advanced security software.
3. Use updated versions of protocols.
4. Implement strong security policies.
5. Use unique and difficult passwords.
6. Ensure strong encrypted communication between client and server.
7. Disable unnecessary ports, protocols, sharing, and default-enabled services.

Chapter 05: Vulnerability Analysis

Introduction
The scanning process includes vulnerability analysis. It is a crucial aspect of the hacking process.

The Concept of Vulnerability Assessment
A penetration tester's primary responsibility is to find weaknesses in an environment. Environmental issues, design flaws, and other security concerns that could lead to the misuse of an operating system, application, or website are all part of vulnerability assessment. They include misconfigurations, default configurations, buffer overflows, Operating System flaws, Open Services, and other flaws.

Vulnerability Assessment
Vulnerability assessment is the process of studying, uncovering, and identifying flaws in systems and applications and evaluating the security mechanisms in place. The ability of the security layer to withstand assaults and exploitations is determined by evaluating the security mechanisms applied in systems and applications. Vulnerability assessment also aids in identifying potentially exploitable flaws, the need for extra security layers, and information that scanners can expose.

Types of Vulnerability Assessment
- Active Assessment
- Passive Assessment
- External Assessment
- Internal Assessment

Vulnerability Assessment Life Cycle
The Vulnerability Assessment life cycle consists of the following phases:
- Creating a Baseline
- Vulnerability Assessment
- Risk Assessment
- Remediation
- Verification
- Monitor

Vulnerability Assessment Solutions
Product-based Solution Vs. Service-based Solution
Product-based solutions are implemented within an organization's corporate network or a private network. Internal (private) networks are frequently the focus of these solutions.

Third-party solutions that provide security and auditing services to a network are known as service-based solutions. These solutions can be hosted on-premises or in the cloud. These third-party solutions pose a security concern since they have access to and monitor the internal network.

Tree-based Assessment Vs. Inference-based Assessment
Tree-based Assessment is an assessment approach in which an auditor follows different strategies for each component of an environment. For example, consider a scenario in which different machines are live on an organization's network—the auditor may employ a different method for Windows-based machines and a different one for Linux-based servers.

Inference-based Assessment is another approach to assessing vulnerabilities depending on the inventory of protocols in an environment. For example, if an auditor finds a protocol using an inference-based assessment approach, he will look for ports and services related to that protocol.

Vulnerability Scoring Systems
Common Vulnerability Scoring System (CVSS)
The Common Vulnerability Scoring System (CVSS) helps diagnose the principal characteristics of a vulnerability and produces a numerical score reflecting its severity. To assist organizations in correctly assessing and prioritizing their vulnerability management activities, the numerical score can be translated into a qualitative representation (low, medium, high, and critical)..

Vulnerability Scanning Tools

Various tools have made detecting vulnerabilities in an existing environment relatively straightforward in this era of current technology and innovation. There are a variety of automatic and manual tools available to assist you in finding vulnerabilities. Vulnerability Scanners are automatic utilities designed to find vulnerabilities, flaws, faults, and loopholes in an Operating System, network, software, and applications. Scripts, open ports, banners, running services, configuration issues, and other areas are all thoroughly examined by these scanning tools.

Vulnerability Assessment Reports

Vulnerability Assessment reports help security teams in addressing the weaknesses and discovered vulnerabilities. VA reports outline all discovered vulnerabilities, weaknesses, security flaws within a network and its connected devices. VA reports should also contain remediation, recommendations, and countermeasures on addressing the outlined security issues.

Chapter 06: System Hacking

System Hacking Methodology

The process of system hacking is classified into System Hacking methods. These methods are also termed CEH hacking methodology by the EC-Council. This methodology includes:

1. Gaining Access
2. Cracking Passwords
3. Vulnerability Exploitation
4. Escalating Privileges
5. Maintaining Access
6. Executing Applications
7. Hiding Files
8. Covering Tracks

Gaining Access

In this phase, an attacker initiates an active connection to intrude into the target's system using the information collected in previous phases. In some cases of reconnaissance or enumeration, the attacker finds enough information or a vulnerability through which they can gain access without any need for a password.

Password Cracking

Before proceeding to Password Cracking, you should know about the three types of authentication factors:

- **Something you know,** such as username/password, security pin, security question, etc.
- **Something you are,** such as biometrics, voice, handwriting, hand geography, face recognition, etc.
- **Something you possess/have,** such as registered/allowed devices, smart cards, RFIDs, etc.

Types of Password Attacks

Password Attacks are classified into the following types:

1. Non-Electronic Attacks
2. Active Online Attacks
3. Passive Online Attacks
4. Default Password
5. Offline Attack

Non-Electronic Attacks

Non-Electronic Attacks or Non-Technical Attacks are those that do not require any type of technical understanding or knowledge. This type of attack can be done by shoulder surfing, social engineering, and dumpster diving.

Active Online Attacks

Active Online Attacks include different techniques that directly interact with the target for cracking the password. Active Online attacks include:

- Dictionary Attack
- Brute Force Attack
- Hash Injection

Passive Online Attacks

Passive Online Attacks are performed without interfering with the target. These are serious attacks because the password is extracted without revealing the information: it obtains the password without directly probing the target. The most common types of Passive Online Attacks are:

- Wire Sniffing
- Man-in-the-Middle Attack
- Replay Attack

Windows Authentication Methods

In computer networking, Authentication is a verification process for identifying any user or device. When you authenticate an entity, the motive of authentication is to validate whether the device is legitimate or not. When you authenticate a user, it means you are verifying the actual user against the imposter.

Vulnerability Exploitation

In cybersecurity, an exploit is also termed a code intended to take advantage of or exploit the vulnerability. These exploits are not only developed by adversaries but also the security researchers as proof of concept. Using these exploit codes specific to each vulnerability, attackers can intrude into a vulnerable system and create persistency.

Escalating Privileges

In Privilege Escalation, there are still many tasks to complete after acquiring access to the target. You may not always have hacked an admin account; sometimes, you have only compromised the user account with lower privileges. Using a compromised account with limited privileges will not help you to achieve your goals. Before anything else, after gaining access, you have to perform privilege escalation to get complete high-level access with no or limited restrictions.

Each Operating System comes with default settings and user accounts, such as administrator account, root account, guest account, etc., with default passwords. It is easy for an attacker to find vulnerabilities in pre-configured accounts in an Operating System to exploit and gain access. To prevent unauthorized access, these default settings and accounts must be secured and modified.

Privilege Escalation is further classified into two types:

1. Horizontal Privileges Escalation
2. Vertical Privileges Escalation

Maintaining Access

After the exploitation and privilege escalation, attackers create a backdoor for later use. Using this backdoor, an attacker can later access the system without any need for exploitation again. Creating a backdoor also eliminates the need for a vulnerability that was exploited to gain access. This way, if the system is later patched, the attacker can still gain access by its created backdoor.

Executing Applications

After gaining unauthorized access to the system and escalating privileges, the attacker's next step is to run malicious software on the target system. This malicious software execution is used to get unauthorized access to system resources, crack passwords, install backdoors, and other purposes. Customized apps or commercial software can be used to create these executable programmes. This application's process/execution is also known as "System Owning." Malicious applications can lead to the following outcomes:

- Installing Malware to collect information
- Installing Cracker to crack passwords and scripts
- Installing Keyloggers to gather information via input devices such as a keyboard

RemoteExec

RemoteExec is software designed for remote installation of an application and execution of code and scripts. Additionally, RemoteExec can update files on the target system across a network.

PDQ Deploy

PDQ Deploy is a software system administrator application that allows you to secretly install and transmit updates to a distant computer. PDQ Deploy enables or facilitates installing programmes and software on a single system or several systems in a network. It can silently deploy almost every application (such as .exe or .msi) to a targeted system. Using PDQ Deploy, you can install or uninstall, copy, execute, and send files.

Keyloggers

Keystroke logging, keylogging, or keyboard capturing is monitoring or recording actions performed by any user.

Spyware

Spyware is software designed for gathering information about a user's interaction with a system, such as an email address, login credentials, and other details, without informing the user of the target system. Mostly, spyware is used for tracking a user's internet interactions. The information obtained is sent to a remote destination. To evade detection, spyware hides its files and processes. Spyware comes in a variety of forms:

- Adware
- System Monitors
- Tracking Cookies
- Trojans

Hiding Files

Rootkits

A rootkit is a collection of software designed to provide a remote user privileged access to a targeted machine. Rootkits are a collection of malicious software that is installed after an attack. When an attacker gains administrative access to a target system and can keep that access in the future, the attacker effectively builds a backdoor. Rootkits frequently hide the existence of their programme to prevent discovery.

NTFS Data Stream

The acronym for NTFS is New Technology File System. The NTFS file system is a proprietary Windows file system developed by Microsoft. NTFS was the default file system in Windows NT 3.1. It is the primary file system of Windows 10, Windows 8, Windows 7, Windows Vista, Windows XP, Windows 2000, and Windows NT..

Alternate Data Stream

In the NTFS file system, Alternate Data Stream (ADS) is a file attribute. This NTFS feature contains metadata that can be used to locate a specific file. For the Macintosh Hierarchical File System, the ADS capability was introduced (HFS). ADS can hide file data within an existing file without causing any obvious modifications. ADS poses a security risk in practice because of its data hiding capabilities, which allows an attacker to hide a malicious piece of data in a file that can be executed when the attacker decides to run.

NTFS Streams Countermeasures

NTFS streams can be secured and protected using third-party tools and approaches. The most basic method for preventing an NTFS stream is moving the file, such as a suspected NTFS stream, to the FAT partition. FAT does not support Alternate Data Stream (ADS). Moving ADS from NTFS to the FAT partition will corrupt the file. Several tools, for example, ADS Spy, ADS Tools, LADS, Stream Armor, etc., can detect and remove malicious alternate data streams completely.

Steganography

Steganography is a technique for ensuring confidentiality by hiding important information in an ordinary transmission. At the destination, a legitimate receiver retrieves secret information. To guarantee confidentiality and integrity, steganography employs encryption. To evade discovery, it also hides encrypted data.

White Space Steganography

White Space Steganography is a technique for hiding information in a text file using extra blank space covering the file inserted between words. Using LZW and Huffman compression methods, the size of the message is decreased.

Steganalysis

Steganalysis is an analysis of suspected information using steganography techniques to discover or retrieve hidden information. Steganalysis inspects any image for encrypted data. Accuracy, efficiency, and noisy samples are the main challenges faced by steganalysis for detecting encrypted data.

Covering Tracks

After gaining access, escalating privileges, and executing the application, the next step is to wipe the evidence. In the Covering Tracks phase, attackers remove all the event logs, error messages, and other evidence that may prevent the attack from being easily discovered.

The most common techniques that attackers often use to cover tracks on the target system are:

- Disabling Auditing
- Clearing Logs
- Manipulating Logs

Chapter 07: Malware Threats

Malware Concepts

Malware is the abbreviation of the term Malicious Software. The term malware is an umbrella term that defines a wide variety of potentially harmful software. This malicious software is specially designed to gain access to target machines, steal information, and harm the target system. Any software designed with the malicious intention that allows damaging, disabling, or limiting the control of the authorized owner and passing control of a target system to a malware developer or attacker, or allows any other malicious intent, can be considered malware. Viruses, Worms, Keyloggers, Spywares, Trojans, Ransomware, and other harmful software are among the many varieties of malware.

Malware Propagation Methods

There are different methods through which malware can get into a system and infect it. Users should be careful while interacting with other devices and the internet. Some of the methods that are still popular for the propagation of malware are:

- Free Software
- File-Sharing Services
- Removable Media
- Email Communication
- Not using a Firewall or Anti-Virus

Trojan Concept

Trojan horse is a malicious program that misleads users about its actual intentions.

Like its namesake, Trojan misleads users about its actual intentions to avoid being detected while scanning and sandboxing and waits for the best time to attack. Trojan may provide unauthorized access to an attacker, as well as access to personal information. Infection of other linked devices over a network is also possible using Trojan.

Trojan

Any Malicious Program misleading the user about its actual intention is classified as a Trojan. Social Engineering typically spreads Trojans. The purpose or most common use of Trojan programs are:

- Creating a Backdoor
- Gaining Unauthorized Access
- Stealing Information
- Infecting Connected Devices
- Ransomware Attacks
- Using Victims for Spamming
- Using Victims as Botnet
- Downloading other Malicious Software
- Disabling Firewalls

Trojan Construction Kit

The Trojan Construction Kit allows attackers to create their own Trojans. These customized Trojans can be more dangerous for the target, as well as the attacker if it backfires or is not executed properly. These Trojans can evade detection by viruses and Trojan scanning software because they were built with construction kits.
Some Trojan Construction Kits are:

- Dark Horse Trojan Virus Maker
- Senna Spy Generator
- Trojan Horse Construction Kit
- Progenic mail Trojan Construction Kit
- Pandora's Box

Droppers

A Dropper is a piece of software or a programme that is dedicated to delivering a payload to the target machine. A dropper's main objective is to silently install malicious codes on a victim's computer, avoiding detection. It spreads and installs malware through a variety of methods.

Trojan-Dropper Tools

- TrojanDropper: Win32/Rotbrow.A
- TrojanDropper: Win32/Swisyn
- Trojan: Win32/Meredrop
- Troj/Destover-C

Wrappers

These are non-malicious files that bind a malicious file to propagate the Trojan. A wrapper binds a malicious file to create and propagate the Trojan along with it to avoid detection. Wrappers are often popular executable files such as games, music, and video files, as well as any other non-malicious file.

Crypters

A Crypter is software used while creating Trojans. The basic purpose of a Crypter is to encrypt, obfuscate, and manipulate malware and malicious programs. Using a Crypter for hiding a malicious program makes it even more difficult for security programs to detect malware. Hackers commonly use them to develop malware that can defeat security programs by posing as a non-malicious program until it is installed.

The following are some of the Crypters that can be used to hide dangerous programs:

- Cryogenic Crypter
- Heaven Crypter
- Swayz Cryptor

Types of Trojans

Command Shell Trojans

Command Shell Trojans are capable of providing remote control of a victim's command shell. Once the Trojan server of the command shell Trojan, such as Netcat, is installed on the target machine, it opens the port for a command shell connection to its client application installed on the attacker's machine. This Client-Server based Trojan provides access to the command line.

Defacement Trojans

Using Defacement Trojans, an attacker can view, edit, and extract information from any Windows program. Using this information, an attacker replaces strings, images, and logos often to leave their mark. They also use User-Styled Custom Application (UCA) to deface programs. Website defacement is well-recognized; it is similar to the concept of applications running on the target machine.

HTTP/HTTPS Trojans

HTTP and HTTPS Trojans bypass the firewall inspection and execute on the target machine. After execution, they create an HTTP/HTTPS tunnel to communicate with the attacker from the victim's machine.

Botnet Trojans

Botnets are the number of compromised systems (zombies). These compromised systems are not limited to any specific LAN; they may be spread over a large geographical area. A Command and Control Center controls these botnets. These botnets are used to launch attacks such as Denial of Service, Spamming, etc.

Proxy Server Trojans

A Trojan-Proxy Server is a standalone malware application that is capable of turning the host system into a proxy server. Proxy Server Trojan allows an attacker to use the victim's computer as a proxy by enabling the victim's system's proxy server. This technique is used to launch further attacks by hiding the actual source of the attack.

Remote Access Trojans (RAT)

Remote Access Trojan (RAT) allows an attacker to get remote desktop access to a victim's computer by enabling Port, allowing GUI access to the remote system. RAT includes a backdoor for maintaining administrative access and control over the victim. Using RAT, an attacker can monitor a user's activity, access confidential information, take screenshots, and record audio and video using a webcam, format drives, and alter files, etc.

Trojan Countermeasures

A network or a system can be protected by following the countermeasures for preventing Trojan attacks. Following are some key countermeasures that can be followed to prevent these attacks and protect your system.

- Avoid clicking on suspect email attachments
- Block unused ports
- Monitor network traffic
- Avoid downloading from untrusted sources
- Install updated security and anti-virus software
- Scan removable media before use
- Verify file integrity
- Enable auditing
- Install a configured host-based firewall
- Install intrusion detection software

Viruses

A virus is self-replicating software that can make numerous copies by attaching itself to another program in any format. These viruses are ready to use as soon as they are downloaded. They can be set to execute in response to a triggering event (waiting for the host to do so) or to sleep for a preset amount of time before executing.

Ransomware

Ransomware is a malware program that restricts access to system files and folders by encrypting them. Some types of ransomware may lock the system as well. Once the system is encrypted, it requires a decryption key to unlock it and its files. An attacker then demands a ransom payment before providing the decryption key to remove restrictions. Online payments using digital currencies that are difficult to trace, like Ukash and Bitcoin, are used for ransoms. Ransomware is normally deployed using Trojans. One of the best examples of ransomware is the WannaCry Ransomware attack.

Following are the most common and widely known types of ransomware:

- Cryptobit Ransomware
- CryptoLocker Ransomware
- CryptoDefense Ransomware
- CryptoWall Ransomware
- Police-themed Ransomware

Types of Viruses

- System or Boot Sector Viruses
- File and Multipartite Viruses
- Macro Viruses
- Cluster Viruses
- Stealth/Tunneling Viruses
- Logic Bombs
- Encryption Virus

Computer Worms

Another sort of malware is worms. Viruses must be activated by an external stimulus, whereas worms may replicate themselves. Worms are unable to attach to other applications. A worm, unlike a virus, can grow and spread across an infected network utilizing File transfer.

Examples of Worms:
- Sobig Worm of 2003
- SQL Slammer Worm of 2003
- 2001 Attacks of Code Red and Nimba
- 2005 Zotob Worm

Virus Analysis and Detection Methods

The Detection phase of a virus initiates with scanning. Initially, the suspected file is scanned for the signature string. In the second step of the detection method, the entire disk is checked for integrity. An integrity checker records the integrity of all files on a disk, usually by calculating the Checksum. If a virus alters a file, it can be detected through an integrity check. In an interception step, requests from the Operating System are monitored. Interception software is used to detect virus-resembling behaviors and to generate a warning for users. Code Emulation and Heuristic Analysis include behavioral analysis and code analysis of a virus by executing it in a sophisticated environment.

Advance Persistent Threat (APT)

Advance Persistent Threats are the most sophisticated threats for an organization. These threats require significant expertise and resources along with the combination of multiple attack vectors. They further require extended foothold and adoption of security controls placed in the target organization to evade and continually exfiltrate the information or achieve motives.

Lazarus Group

Lazarus Associated Groups
- HIDDEN COBRA
- Guardians of Peace
- ZINC
- NICKEL ACADEMY

Cobalt Group

Cobalt Group is another well-known APT group. It is categorized as a financially motivated threat that targets ATMs, payment card systems, SWIFT systems, and other related payment schemes. Cobalt Group targeted banks are Eastern Europe, Central Asia, and Southeast Asia. This group is still active after the arrest of an alleged leader in Spain.

Cobalt group is known for its worldwide bank targets, attacking more than 100 banks across 40 countries. Security researchers believe that the arrest of one of the leaders of the Cobalt group splits the Cobalt group in Cobalt Gang 1.0 and Cobalt 2.0. Cobalt 1.0 extensively uses Threadkit builder for attack techniques, whereas

Cobalt 2.0 became even more sophisticated using APT28 (fancy bear) and MuddyWater.

Cobalt Associated Groups
- Cobalt Gang
- Cobalt Spider

Fileless Malware

Fileless malware is another emerging threat to organizations. It uses legitimate programs such as CMD or PowerShell to infect a computer system. The concept of being file-less is that it does not bring any file to the target system. It does not rely on files, making it more challenging to detect and remove. Fileless malware emerged in 2017. The most recent attacks of Fileless malware are the Hack of the Democratic National Committee and Equifix breach.

Characteristics of Fileless Malware
- Leverages approved applications that are already on the targeted system
- Traditional AV solutions can detect no identifiable code or signature
- Heuristics scanners can detect no particular behavior
- Memory-based: lives in system memory
- Uses processes that are built into the operating system
- It can be paired with other types of malware
- May remain in the environment despite whitelisting and sandboxing measures

Malware Reverse Engineering

Sheep Dipping

Sheep Dipping analyzes a suspect file and packets against viruses and malware before allowing them to be available for users in an isolated environment. This analysis is performed on a dedicated computer. This initial line of defense runs with highly secure computing and port monitoring, file monitoring, anti-viruses, and other security programs.

Malware Analysis

Malware Analysis is the process of identifying malware and ensuring that the malware is completely removed. This process includes observing the behavior of malware, scoping the potential threat to a system, and finding other measures. Before explaining the malware analysis, the need for malware analysis and the goal of this analytics must be defined. Security analysts and security professionals, at some point in their careers, have all performed malware analysis. The major goal of malware analysis is to gain detailed information and observe malware's behavior, maintain incident response, and take defensive actions to secure the organization.

Goals of Malware Analysis

Malware analysis goals are defined below:

- Diagnostics of threat severity or level of attack
- Diagnostics of the type of malware
- Scope the attack's impact
- Built defense to secure organization's network and systems
- Find a root cause
- Built incident response actions
- Develop anti-malware

Chapter 08: Sniffing

Sniffing Concept

Sniffing is the process of scanning and monitoring captured data packets passing through a network by using sniffers. The process of sniffing is carried out by using Promiscuous Ports. Enabling promiscuous mode function on the connected network interface allows capturing all traffic, even when the traffic is not intended for them. Once the packet is captured, you can easily perform the inspection.

There are two types of Sniffing:

1. Active Sniffing
2. Passive Sniffing

Passive Sniffing

Passive Sniffing is the type of sniffing in which there is no need to send additional packets or involve a device, such as a hub, to receive packets. As we know, the hub broadcasts every packet to its port, which helps the attacker to monitor all traffic passing through a hub with no effort.

Active Sniffing

Active Sniffing is the type of sniffing in which an attacker has to send additional packets to the connected device, such as a Switch, to start receiving packets. As we know, a unicast packet from the switch is transmitted to a specific port only. The attacker uses certain techniques such as MAC Flooding, DHCP Attacks, DNS poisoning, Switch Port Stealing, ARP Poisoning, and Spoofing to monitor traffic passing through the switch.

Hardware Protocol Analyzer

Protocol Analyzers, either hardware or software, analyze the captured packets and signals over the transmission channel. Hardware Protocol Analyzers are the physical equipment that captures the packets without interfering with network traffic. Major advantages offered by these hardware protocol analyzers are mobility, flexibility, and throughput. Using these hardware analyzers, an attacker can:

- Monitor network usage
- Identify traffic from hacking software
- Decrypt the packets
- Extract the information
- Modify the size of the packet

SPAN Port

You have a user who has complained about network performance while no one else in the building is experiencing the same issue. You want to run a Network Analyzer on the port, like Wireshark, to monitor ingress and egress traffic. To do this, you can configure SPAN (Switch Port Analyzer). SPAN allows you to capture traffic from one port to another port on the same switch.

Wiretapping

Wiretapping is gaining information by tapping the signal from wires such as telephone lines or the internet. Usually, wiretapping is performed by a third party to monitor conversations. Wiretapping is basically an electrical tap on a telephone line. Legal Wiretapping is known as Legal Interception, which is mostly performed by governmental or security agencies.

Wiretapping is classified into two types:

- Active Wiretapping
- Passive Wiretapping

Lawful Interception

Lawful Interception (LI) is a process of wiretapping with a legal authorization that allows law enforcement agencies to selectively wiretap the communication of an individual user. The standard organization of the telecommunication sector standardized the legal interception gateways for agencies' interception of communication.

Planning Tool for Resource Integration (PRISM)

PRISM stands for Planning Tool for Resource Integration Synchronization and Management. PRISM is a tool specially designed to collect the information passing through American servers.

MAC Attacks

MAC Address Table/CAM Table

MAC is the abbreviation of Media Access Control. A MAC address is the physical address of a device. It is a 48-bit unique identification number assigned to a network device for communication at a data-link layer. A MAC address comprises a 24-bit Object Unique Identifier (OUI) and 24-bit Network Interface Controller (NIC). In cases of multiple NICs, the device will have multiple unique MAC addresses.

MAC Flooding

MAC flooding is a technique in which an attacker sends random MAC addresses mapped with random IP to overflow the storage capacity of a CAM table. A switch then acts as a hub because a CAM table has a fixed length. It will now broadcast the packet on all ports, which helps an attacker sniff the packet with ease. A Unix/Linux utility, known as **"macof"**, offers MAC flooding. Using macof, a random source MAC and IP can be sent to an interface.

Switch Port Stealing

Switch Port Stealing is a packet sniffing technique that employs the usage of MAC flooding to sniff packets.

Defending Against MAC Attacks

Port Security is used to secure the ports. You can bind a known MAC address with a port (static) or specify the limit to learn the MAC on a port (dynamic). You can also enforce a violation action on a port. Hence, if an attacker tries to connect his PC or embedded device to the switch port, the port is configured to support a specific MAC address only.

DHCP Attacks

Dynamic Host Configuration Protocol (DHCP) Operation

DHCP is the method of dynamically allocating IP addresses to be assigned automatically and can be reused when hosts are not using them. The round trip time is the time between discovering the DHCP server and receiving the leased IP address. RTT can be used to evaluate DHCP's performance. Because it does not have information about the network to which it is connected, a DHCP client uses UDP broadcast to deliver an initial DHCP-Discover packet. The DHCP server responds with a DHCP-Offer Packet, which contains the configuration parameters, to the DHCP-Discover packet. A DHCP-Request packet will be sent from the DHCP client to the DHCP server requesting configuration parameters. Finally, the DHCP server will send the DHCP-Acknowledgement packet containing configuration parameters.

DHCPv4 uses two different ports:

- UDP port 67 for Server
- UDP port 68 for Client

DHCP Starvation Attack

A denial-of-service attack against a DHCP server is known as a DHCP starvation attack. An attacker uses faked MAC addresses to send bogus requests for broadcasting to a DHCP server in order to lease all IP addresses in the DHCP address pool in a DHCP Starvation attack. Following the allocation of all IP addresses, new users will be unable to receive an IP address or renew their lease.

Rogue DHCP Server Attack

The rogue DHCP server is deployed in the network coupled with the Starvation attack in a Rogue DHCP Server Attack. When a lawful DHCP server is attacked with a denial-of-service attack, DHCP clients cannot obtain IP addresses from that server. A phoney DHCP server responds to incoming DHCP Discovery (IPv4) or Solicit (IPv6) packets with a configuration option that directs traffic towards it.

ARP Poisoning

Address Resolution Protocol (ARP)

ARP is a stateless protocol used within a broadcast domain to ensure communication by resolving the IP address to MAC address mapping. It is in charge of L3 to L2 address mappings. ARP protocol ensures the binding of IP addresses and MAC addresses.

ARP Spoofing Attack

In ARP spoofing, an attacker sends forged ARP packets over a Local Area Network (LAN). In this case, the switch will update the attacker's MAC Address with the IP address of a legitimate user or server. Once an attacker's MAC address is learned, together with the IP address of an authentic user, the switch will start forwarding the packets to the attacker, assuming that it is the MAC of the user. Using an ARP Spoofing attack, an attacker can steal information by extracting it from the packet intended for a user over LAN that it received. Apart from stealing information, ARP spoofing can be used for:

- Session Hijacking
- Denial-of-Service Attack
- Man-in-the-Middle Attack
- Packet Sniffing
- Data Interception
- Connection Hijacking
- VoIP Tapping
- Connection Resetting
- Stealing Passwords

Defending ARP Poisoning

Dynamic ARP Inspection (DAI)

DAI is used with DHCP snooping. ARP is a Layer 2 protocol that functions on IP-to-MAC bindings. Dynamic ARP Inspection (DAI) is a security feature that validates ARP packets within a network. DAI investigates the ARP packets by intercepting, logging, and discarding the invalid IP-MAC address bindings. To build the MAC-to-IP bindings for DAI validation, DHCP snooping is required.

Spoofing Attack

MAC Spoofing/Duplicating

MAC Spoofing is manipulating a MAC address to impersonate the authentic user or launch attacks such as denial-of-service. A MAC address is built on a network interface controller that cannot be changed, but some drivers enable changing the MAC address. This masking process of MAC addresses is known as MAC Spoofing.

MAC Spoofing Tool

There are several tools available that offer MAC spoofing with ease. Some popular tools are:

- Technitium MAC Address Changer
- SMAC

DNS Poisoning

DNS Poisoning Techniques

Domain Name System (DNS) is an important protocol used in networking to maintain records and translate human-readable domain names into IP addresses. When a DNS server receives a request, it translates the human-readable domain name, such as "google.com", into its mapped IP address. When it does not find the mapping translation in its database, it generates the query to another DNS server for translation. The DNS server with the translation will reply to the requesting DNS server, and the client's query will be resolved.

Intranet DNS Spoofing

Intranet DNS spoofing is usually done on a switched network over a local area network (LAN). The attacker performs intranet DNS spoofing via the ARP poisoning technique. Attackers sniff the packet, extract the ID of DNS requests, and respond with a bogus IP translation that redirects traffic to a malicious website. Before the authentic DNS server can resolve the query, the attacker must be quick enough to react.

Internet DNS Spoofing

Internet DNS Spoofing is performed by replacing the DNS configuration on the target machine. All DNS queries will be directed to a malicious DNS server controlled by the attacker, directing the traffic to malicious sites. Typically, internet DNS spoofing is accomplished by infecting the target with a Trojan and modifying the DNS setup to route searches toward them.

Proxy Server DNS Poisoning

Similar to internet DNS Spoofing, Proxy Server DNS poisoning is performed by replacing the DNS configuration from the web browser. All web queries are directed to a malicious proxy server controlled by the attacker, redirecting traffic to malicious sites.

DNS Cache Poisoning

Normally, internet users use DNS provided by the Internet Service Provider (ISP). In a corporate network, the organization uses its own DNS servers to improve performance by caching frequently or previously generated queries. DNS Cache poisoning is performed by exploiting flaws in the DNS software. An attacker adds or alters the entries in the DNS record cache, which redirects traffic to the malicious site. When an internal DNS server is unable to validate the DNS response from the authoritative DNS server, it updates the entry locally to entertain the user requests.

Sniffing Tools

Wireshark

Wireshark is the most popular and widely used Network Protocol Analyzer tool across commercial, governmental, non-profit, and educational organizations. It is a free, open-source tool available natively for Windows, Linux, MAC, BSD, Solaris, and other platforms. Wireshark also offers a terminal version called TShark.

Sniffing Detection Techniques

Ping Method

The Ping technique is used to detect a sniffer. A ping request is sent to the suspect IP address with a spoofed MAC address. If the NIC is not running in promiscuous mode, it will not respond to the packet. In cases where the suspect is running a sniffer, it will respond to the packet. This is an older technique and is not very reliable.

ARP Method

Using ARP, sniffers can be detected with the help of the ARP Cache. By sending a non-broadcast ARP packet to the sniffer, the MAC address will be cached if the NIC is running in promiscuous mode. The next step is to send a broadcast ping with a spoofed MAC address. If the machine is running in promiscuous mode, it replies to the packets of the known MAC address from the sniffed non-broadcasted ARP packets.

Promiscuous Detection Tool

Promiscuous Detection tools such as **PromqryUI** or **Nmap** can also be used to detect a Network Interface Card running in Promiscuous Mode. These tools are GUI-based application software.

Chapter 09: Social Engineering

Social Engineering Concepts

Social Engineering is the act of stealing information from humans. It does not require any interaction with target systems or networks, so it is considered a non-technical attack. Social Engineering is seen as the art of convincing the target to reveal and share information. This may be done through physical interaction with the target or by convincing the target to part with information using any social media platform. This technique is much easier than others because people are careless and often unaware of the importance and value of their information.

Vulnerabilities Leading to Social Engineering Attacks

"Trust" is a major vulnerability that leads to social engineering attacks. Humans trust each other and do not secure their credentials from their close ones, leading to an attack. A second person may reveal information to a third, or a third person may shoulder surf to obtain information.

Phases of a Social Engineering Attack

Social Engineering Attacks are not complex, nor do they require strong technical knowledge – an attacker might be a non-technical person, as defined earlier. It is an act of stealing information from people. However, social engineering attacks are performed by following the steps.

Research

The Research phase includes collecting information about a target organization. It may be collected through dumpster diving, scanning an organization's website, finding information on the internet, gathering information from employees, etc.

Select Target

In selecting a target phase, an attacker selects the target among other employees of an organization. A frustrated target is preferable as it is usually easier to extract information from such a person.

Relationship

The Relationship phase consists of creating a relationship with the target so that the target is unable to identify the real intentions of the attacker. The target should completely trust the attacker.

Exploit

In this stage, the attacker exploits the relationship by collecting sensitive information such as username, passwords, network information, etc.

Social Engineering Techniques

Social Engineering attacks can be performed through different techniques, which are classified into the following types:

Human-based Social Engineering

Human-based Social Engineering includes one-to-one interaction with the target. A social engineer gathers sensitive information by tricking the target by ensuring a level of trust, taking advantage of habits, behavior, and moral obligations. Some features include:

- Impersonation
- Eavesdropping and Shoulder Surfing
- Dumpster Diving
- Reverse Social Engineering
- Piggybacking and Tailgating

Computer-based Social Engineering

There are different ways to perform computer-based social engineering. Pop-up windows requiring login credentials, internet messaging, and emails such as Hoax letters, Chain letters, and Spam are the most popular methods.

- Phishing
- Spear Phishing

Mobile-based Social Engineering

- Publishing Malicious Apps
- Repackaging Legitimate Apps
- Fake Security Apps

Insider Attack

Social Engineering does not only refer to a third person gathering information about your organization. It may be an insider, an employee of your organization with or without privileges, spying on your organization for malicious intentions. Insider attacks are those attacks conducted by these insiders, who may be supported by a competitor of the organization hoping to obtain secrets and other sensitive information.

Hoaxes

This type of threat is when an organization is warned of a particular problem and then asked for money to solve or remove it. These types of threats can be sent through email, Facebook posts, or tweets; the aim is to make money by fooling others.

Watering Hole Attacks

These attacks are carried out when the security inside an organization is extremely strong; attackers cannot get inside the network and attack the security system using threats.

Impersonation on Social Networking Sites

Social Engineering through Impersonation on Social Networking Sites

Impersonation on social networking sites is very popular, easy, and interesting. The malicious user gathers a target's personal information from different sources, mostly from social networking sites. The gathered information may include the full name, a recent profile picture, the date of birth, residential address, email address, contact details, professional details, educational details, etc.

Risks of Social Networking to Corporate Networks

A social networking site is not as secure as a corporate site. The authentication, identification, and authorization of an employee accessing resources on these sites are different. For example, logging into a bank account through a website and logging into a social media account has different security levels. Social networking sites do not carry sensitive information; hence they follow ordinary authentication. The major weakness of social networking is its vulnerability in authentication. An attacker can easily manipulate the security authentication and create a fake account to access information.

Identity Theft

Identity theft is stealing information about the identity of another person. Identity theft is popularly used in fraud. Anyone with malicious intent may steal your identity by gathering documents such as utility bills, personal and other relevant information and create a new ID card to impersonate someone. This information may also be used to confirm the fake identity and then take advantage of it.

Social Engineering Countermeasures

Social Engineering Attacks can be mitigated through several methods. Privacy in the corporate environment is necessary to prevent shoulder surfing and dumpster diving threats. Configuring strong passwords, securing passwords, and keeping them secret will protect against social engineering. Social networking platforms are always at risk of information leakage. Yet social networks are an increasingly important part of an organization's marketing, so keeping an eye on social networking platforms, logging, training, awareness, and audits are necessary to reduce the risk of social engineering attacks.

Chapter 10: Denial-of-Service (DoS)

DoS/DDoS Concepts

A Denial-of-Service (DoS) attack on a system or network results in either denial of service or services, a reduction in functions and operation of that system, prevention of legitimate users accessing the resources. In short, a DoS attack on a service or network makes it unavailable for legitimate users. The DoS attack technique is to generates huge traffic to the target system requesting a specific service. This unexpected amount of traffic overloads the system's capacity and results in a system crash or unavailability.

Common symptoms of DoS attacks are:

- Slow performance
- Increase in spam emails
- Unavailability of a resource
- Loss of access to a website
- Disconnection of a wireless or wired internet connection
- Denial of access to any internet service

Distributed Denial-of-Service (DDoS)

DDoS is similar to Denial-of-Service in that an attacker generates fake traffic. In a Distributed DoS attack, multiple compromised systems attack a target to cause a denial of service. Botnets are used for carrying out a DDoS attack.

DoS/DDoS Attack Techniques

Volumetric Attacks

Volumetric Attacks focus on overloading bandwidth consumption capabilities. These volumetric attacks are carried out to slow down the performance and degrade the service. Typically, these attacks consume hundreds of Gbps of bandwidth.

Fragmentation Attacks

DoS Fragmentation Attacks fragment the IP datagram into multiple smaller size packets. These fragmented packets require reassembling at the destination, requiring the router's resources. Fragmentation attacks are of the following two types:

1. UDP and ICMP Fragmentation Attacks
2. TCP Fragmentation Attacks

TCP-State-Exhaustion Attacks

TCP State-Exhaustion Attacks focus on web servers, firewalls, load balancers, and other infrastructure components to disrupt connections by consuming the connection state tables. A TCP State-Exhaustion attack results in exhausting the finite number of concurrent connections the target device can support. The most common state-exhaustion attack is the ping of death.

Application Layer Attacks

An Application Layer DDoS Attack is also called a layer 7 DDoS attack. An application-level DoS attack focuses on the application layer of the OSI model for its malicious intention. An application-layer DDoS attack includes an HTTP flood attack in which a victim's server is attacked by botnets flooding it with HTTP requests.

Bandwidth Attacks

A bandwidth Attack requires multiple sources to generate a request to overload the target. A DoS attack using a single machine is not capable of generating enough requests to overwhelm the service. The distributed DoS attack is a very effective technique for flooding requests toward a target.

Service Request Floods

A Service Request Flood is a DoS attack in which an attacker floods requests to a server, such as an application server or web server until the entire service is overloaded. When a legitimate user attempts to initiate a connection, it will be denied because the TCP connections limit on the server has already been exceeded (with fake TCP requests generated by an attacker to consume all resources to the point of exhaustion).

SYN Attack/Flooding

SYN Attacks or SYN Flooding exploit the three-way handshake. The attacker floods SYN requests to the target server, intending to tie up the system.

ICMP Flood Attack

Another DoS attack that leverages ICMP queries is an Internet Control Message Protocol (ICMP) Flood Attack. ICMP is a network device support protocol that sends operational data, error messages, and indications. These requests and responses consume the network device's resources. As a result, flooding ICMP requests without waiting for responses exhausts the device's resources.

Peer-to-Peer Attacks

A Peer-to-Peer DDoS Attack exploits bugs in peer-to-peer servers or peering technology by using the Direct Connect (DC++) protocol to execute a DDoS attack. Most peer-to-peer networks are on the DC++ client.

Permanent Denial-of-Service Attack

A Permanent Denial-of-Service Assault is a DoS attack that focuses on hardware sabotage rather than denial of service. When a PDoS assault occurs, the hardware is damaged to the point that it must be replaced or reinstalled. PDoS is carried out through Phlashing, which causes irreversible hardware damage or Bricking a system by delivering bogus hardware updates.

Application Level Flood Attacks

Application Level Attacks focus on layer 7 of the OSI model. These attacks target the application server or application running on a client computer. An attacker finds faults and flaws in an application or Operating System and exploits the vulnerabilities to bypass the access control—gaining complete control over the application, system, or network.

Distributed Reflection Denial-of-Service (DRDoS)

A Distributed Reflection Denial-of-Service Assault (DRDoS) is a DoS attack in which secondary and intermediary victims are used to initiate the attack. An attacker makes requests to the intermediary victim, who then routes traffic to the secondary target. The traffic is redirected to the target via the secondary victim. The use of intermediary and secondary victims is intended to deceive the attacker.

Botnets

Botnets are used to carry out a task indefinitely. These botnets use malicious scripts and codes to gain access to a system. When the botnets take control of the system, this alerts the master computer. An attacker can use this master machine to control the system and submit requests to launch a DoS attack.

Botnet Setup

The Botnet is usually set up by utilizing Trojan Horse to install a bot on a victim. The payload of a Trojan Horse is a bot, which is transmitted to the victim via phishing or redirection to either a malicious or a compromised legitimate website. The device becomes infected and under the control of Bot Command and Control once this malicious payload is run (C&C). Through Handler, C&C has control over all compromised devices. The handler connects the infected device to C&S and waits for orders to send the zombies after the principal target.

Scanning Vulnerable Machines

Several techniques are used for scanning vulnerable machines, including Random, Hit-list, Topological, Subnet, and Permutation Scanning.

Propagation of Malicious Code

There are three common methods for spreading harmful code. They are as follows:
1. Central Source Propagation
2. Back-Chaining Propagation
3. Autonomous Propagation

Botnet Trojan

- Blackshades NET
- Cythosia Botnet and Andromeda Bot
- PlugBot

DoS/DDoS Attack Tools

Pandora DDoS Bot Toolkit

The Pandora DDoS Toolkit was developed by Sokol, who also developed the Dirt Jumper Toolkit. The Pandora DDoS Toolkit can generate five types of attacks, including infrastructure and application-layer attacks, namely:
1. HTTP Min
2. HTTP Download
3. HTTP Combo
4. Socket Connect

5. Max Flood

Other DDoS Attack Tools
- Derail
- HOIC
- DoS HTTP
- BanglaDos

DoS and DDoS Attack Tools for Mobile
- AnDOSid
- Low Orbit Ion Cannon (LOIC)

Countermeasures

There are several methods for detecting and preventing DoS/DDoS assaults. Some of the most often utilized security techniques are as follows:

Activity Profiling

Activity Profiling means monitoring the activities running on a system or network. DoS/DDoS attacks can be observed by analyzing a packet's header information for TCP Sync, UDP, ICMP, and Netflow traffic by monitoring the traffic flow. Activity profiling is measured by comparing it to the average traffic rate of a network.

Wavelet Analysis

Wavelet-based Signal Analysis is an automated procedure that analyses input signals to detect DoS/DDoS attacks. Volume-based anomalies are detected using this automated detection. Adaptive threshold approaches identify DoS attacks, whereas Wavelet analysis analyses traffic and filters it on a scale.

Sequential Change-Point Detection

Change-Point detection is an algorithm used to detect denial-of-service (DoS) attacks. This detection technique uses a non-parametric Cumulative Sum (CUSUM) algorithm to detect traffic patterns. Change-Point detection requires very low computational overheads. The Sequential Change-Point detection algorithm isolates the changes in the network traffic statistics caused by the attack. Key functions of the sequential change-point detection technique are to:

1. Isolate Traffic
2. Filter Traffic
3. Identify an Attack
4. Identify Scan Activity

Techniques to Defend against Botnets

RFC 3704 Filtering

Filtering according to RFC 3704 is used to protect against botnets. To limit DDoS attacks, RFC 3704 is developed for ingress filtering for multi-homed networks. It blocks access to the network for traffic with a faked address and traces the host's source address.

Cisco IPS Source IP Reputation Filtering

Source IP Reputation Filtering is ensured by Cisco IPS devices, which can filter traffic based on reputation score and other factors. IPS devices collect real-time information from a Sensor Base Network. Its Global Correlation feature ensures the intelligence update of known threats, including botnets and malware, to help in detecting advanced and latest threats. These threat intelligence updates are frequently downloaded on IPS and Cisco firepower devices.

Black Hole Filtering

Black Hole Filtering is a process of silently dropping traffic (either incoming or outgoing) so that the source is not notified about a packet being discarded. Remotely Triggered Black Hole Filtering (RTBHF) is a routing technique and is used to mitigate DoS attacks by using the Border Gateway Protocol (BGP). The router performs black hole filtering using null-0 interfaces. However, BGP also supports blackhole filtering.

Enabling TCP Intercept on Cisco IOS Software

The TCP Intercept command is used on Cisco IOS routers to protect TCP Servers from TCP SYN flooding attacks. The TCP Intercept feature prevents the TCP SYN, a type of DoS attack, by intercepting and validating TCP connections. Incoming TCP Synchronization (SYN) packets are matched against the extended access list. TCP intercept software responds to TCP connection requests on behalf of the destination server; if the connection is successful, it establishes a session with the destination server on behalf of the requesting client and transparently knits the connection together. As a result, SYN flooding will never reach the target server.

Chapter 11: Session Hijacking

Introduction

The concept of session hijacking is an interesting topic for several different scenarios. It is the hijacking of sessions by intercepting the communication between hosts. The attacker usually intercepts communications to take on the role of an authenticated user or to carry out a "Man-in-the-Middle" attack.

Session Hijacking Concept

To understand the concept of session hijacking, consider an authenticated TCP session between two hosts. The attacker intercepts the session and takes it over. When the session's authentication process is complete, the user can use resources such as web services, TCP communication, etc. The attacker takes advantage of this authenticated session and places him/herself between the authenticated user and the host. The authentication process initiates only at the start of a TCP session; once the attacker successfully bypasses the authentication of a TCP session, the session will have been hijacked. Session hijacking is successful when there are weak IDs or no blockage when receiving an invalid ID.

Session Hijacking Techniques

Following are the techniques of session hijacking:

Stealing

There are various techniques for stealing a session ID, such as Referrer Attack, Network Sniffing, Trojans, etc.

Guessing

Observing the changeable components of session IDs or determining the legitimate session ID by working out the sequence, are examples of tactics and strategies used to predict the session ID.

Brute-Forcing

The process of brute-forcing involves guessing every conceivable combination of credentials. When an attacker has gotten information about the session ID range, it is frequently used.

The Session Hijacking Process

The process of session hijacking involves:

Sniffing

An attacker attempts to place himself between the victim and the target to sniff the packet.

Monitoring

An attacker monitors the traffic flow between the victim and the target.

Session Desynchronization

This is the process of breaking the connection between the victim and the target.

Session ID

An attacker takes control of the session by predicting the session ID.

Command Injection

After successfully taking control of the session, the attacker starts inserting commands.

Types of Session Hijacking

Active Attack

An Active Attack involves the attacker actively intercepting the active session. In an active attack, the attacker may send packets to the host. In this type of attack, the attacker manipulates the legitimate users of the connection. Once an active attack is successful, the legitimate user becomes disconnected from the attacker.

Passive Attack

A passive attack involves hijacking a session and monitoring the communication between hosts without sending any packets.

Session Hijacking in OSI Model

Network Level Hijacking

Network Level Hijacking involves hijacking a network layer session such as a TCP or UDP session.

Application Level Hijacking

Application Level Hijacking involves hijacking an Application layer such as an HTTPS session.

Spoofing vs. Hijacking

The main distinction between Spoofing and Hijacking is the presence of an active session. In a spoofing attack, the attacker pretends to be someone else in order to obtain access. The attacker does not have any active sessions but uses stolen information to start a new one with the target.

Hijacking is the act of seizing control of an active session between an authenticated user and a specific host. Without creating a new session with the target, the attacker leverages the authorized, legitimate user's session.

Application Level Session Hijacking

Session hijacking focuses on the application layer of the OSI model. In the application layer hijacking process, the attacker is looking for a legitimate session ID from the victim to gain access to an authenticated session that allows the attacker to use web resources. With application layer hijacking, an attacker can access the website resources secured for the use of authenticated users. The web server may assume that the incoming requests are from a known host when the session has been hijacked by an attacker, usually by predicting the session ID.

Compromising Session IDs using Sniffing

Sniffing for the session ID/Token is a sniffing technique in which an attacker hunts for it. The attacker can acquire access to the resources once he discovers the session ID.

Compromising Session IDs by Predicting Session Token

Observing a client's currently occupied session IDs is the method of predicting session ID. An attacker can guess the next session key by observing common and variable elements of the session key.

Compromising Session IDs Using a Man-in-the-Middle Attack

To compromise the session ID via a Man-in-the-Middle attack, the victim's connection to the web server must be split into two different connections, one between the victim and the attacker and the other between the attacker and the server.

Compromising Session IDs Using a Man-in-the-Browser Attack

A Trojan must be installed on the target machine to compromise a session ID using a Man-in-the-Browser attack. The Trojan can alter proxy settings or force all traffic to go via the attacker. Intercepting the process between the browser and its security mechanism is another Trojan approach.

Compromising Session IDs Using Client-side Attacks

Session IDs can be compromised easily by using Client-side attacks such as:

1. Cross-Site Scripting (XSS)
2. Malicious JavaScript Code
3. Trojans

Cross-site Script Attacks

An attacker performs a Cross-site Scripting Attack by sending a crafted link with a malicious script. When the user clicks the malicious link, the script is executed. This script might be coded to extract and send the session IDs to the attacker.

Cross-site Request Forgery Attack

A Cross-site Request Forgery (CSRF) attack is the process of obtaining a legitimate user's session ID and exploiting the active session with the trusted website in order to perform malicious activities.

Session Replay Attack

Another technique for session hijacking is the Session Replay Attack. Attackers capture from users the authentication token intended for the server and replay the request to the server, resulting in unauthorized access to the server.

Session Fixation

Session Fixation is an attack permitting the attacker to hijack the session. The attacker has to provide a valid session ID and make a victim's browser use it. The following techniques do this:

1. Session Token in the URL argument
2. Session Token in hidden form
3. Session ID in a cookie

Network Level Session Hijacking

The Transport layer and Internet layer protocols utilized by the application layer are the focus of Network Level

Hijacking. A network-level assault retrieves data that could be used in an application layer session.

There are several types of network-level hijacking, including:

- Blind Hijacking
- UDP Hijacking
- TCP/IP Hijacking
- RST Hijacking
- MITM
- IP Spoofing

The Three-Way Handshake

TCP communication initiates with a three-way handshake between the requesting and the target host. In this handshake, Synchronization (SYN) packets and Acknowledgment (ACK) packets are communicated.

TCP/IP Hijacking

The TCP/IP Hijacking process is a network-level attack on a TCP session in which an attacker predicts the sequence number of a packet flowing between the victim and host. To perform a TCP/IP attack, the attacker must be on the same network as the victim. Usually, the attacker uses sniffing tools to capture the packets and extract the sequence number. By injecting the spoofed packet, the attacker can interrupt a session. Communication with the legitimate user can be disrupted by a denial-of-service attack or a reset connection.

Source Routing

Source routing is a technique of sending a packet via a selected route. In session hijacking, this technique is used to attempt IP spoofing as a legitimate host with the help of source routing to direct traffic through a path identical to the victim's path.

RST Hijacking

RST hijacking is the process of sending a Reset (RST) packet to the victim with a spoofed source address. The acknowledgment number used in this reset packet is also predicted. When the victim receives this packet, he/she will not be aware that the packet is spoofed. The victim resets the connection assuming that an actual source requested the connection reset request. An RST packet can be crafted using packet designing tools.

Blind Hijacking

Blind Hijacking is a technique used when an attacker is unable to capture the return traffic. In blind hijacking, the attacker captures a packet coming from the victim and heading toward the server, injects a malicious packet, and forwards it to the targeted server.

Forged ICMP and ARP Spoofing

A Forged ICMP Packet and ARP Spoofing techniques can also be used to launch a man-in-the-middle attack. To deceive the victim, forged ICMP packets such as destination unavailable or high latency messages are generated.

UDP Hijacking

The UDP Session Hijacking process is simpler than TCP session hijacking. Since the UDP is a connectionless protocol, it does not require any sequence packet between the requesting client and host. UDP session hijacking is all about sending a response packet before the destination server responds. There are several techniques to intercept the coming traffic from the destination server.

Session Hijacking Countermeasures

There are several detection techniques and countermeasures that can be implemented to mitigate session hijacking attacks. These can be manual or automated. Deployment of defense-in-depth technology and network monitoring devices such as Intrusion Detection System (IDS) and Intrusion Prevention System (IPS) are automated detection processes. For manual detection, there are several packet sniffing tools available.

IPSec

IPsec stands for Internet Protocol Security. It is used to secure generic IP traffic, as the name suggests. IPsec's strength comes in its flexibility to support a variety of protocols and algorithms. It also contains new encryption and hashing protocol advances. The primary goal of IPsec is to offer CIA (Confidentiality, Integrity, and Authentication) for virtual networks in today's networks.

Components of IPsec

Components of IPsec include:

- IPsec Drivers
- Internet Key Exchange (IKE)

- Internet Security Association Key Management Protocol
- Oakley
- IPsec Policy Agent

Modes of IPsec

IPsec has two modes of operation: tunnel and transport. Each has its own characteristics and processes for execution.

IIPsec Tunnel Mode

Tunnel mode, the default option in Cisco equipment, shields the entire IP packet from the source device. This means that a new packet with a different IP header is produced and transmitted to the untrusted network and VPN peer for each original packet. Tunnel mode is often used in Site-to-Site VPNs when two secure IPsec gateways are joined via an IPsec VPN connection across the public internet.

IPsec Transport Mode

In transport mode, the IPsec VPN secures the data field or payload of the originating IP traffic using encryption, hashing, or both. New IPsec headers encapsulate only the payload field while the original IP headers remain unchanged. Tunnel mode is used when original IP packets are the source and destination address of secure IPsec peers.

Chapter 12: Evading IDS, Firewalls, and Honeypots

Introduction

Awareness of cyber and network security is increasing day by day. It is very important to understand the core concepts of the Intrusion Detection/Defense System (IDS) and the Intrusion Prevention System (IPS). IDS and IPS often create confusion as multiple vendors create both modules and use similar terminology to define the technical concepts. Sometimes the same technology is used for the detection and prevention of threats.

Like other producers, Cisco has developed several solutions for implementing IDS/IPS for network security. The first part of this section will discuss different concepts before moving on to the different implementation methodologies.

Intrusion Detection Systems (IDS)

The main differentiation between IPS and IDS is the placement of sensors within a network. A sensor can be placed in line with the network, i.e., the common in/out of a specific network segment terminates on a sensor's hardware or logical interface and goes out from a sensor's second piece of hardware or logical interface.

Ways to Detect an Intrusion

When a sensor is analyzing traffic for something strange, it uses multiple techniques based on the rules defined in the IPS/IDS sensor. The following tools and techniques can be used in this regard:

- Signature-based IDS/IPS
- Policy-based IDS/IPS
- Anomaly-based IDS/IPS
- Reputation-based IDS/IPS

Types of Intrusion Detection Systems

IDS/IPS modules are deployed in one of the following configurations, depending on the network scenario:

- Host-based Intrusion Detection
- Network-based Intrusion Detection

Host-based IPS/IDS is typically used to defend a single host machine, and it interacts closely with the kernel of that machine's operating system. It creates a filtering layer that blocks any malicious application from accessing the operating system. There are four major types of Host-based IDS/IPS:

- File System Monitoring
- Log Files Analysis
- Connection Analysis
- Kernel Level Detection

Firewall

The primary function of using a dedicated firewall at the edge of a corporate network is isolation. A firewall prevents the internal LAN from having a direct connection with the internet or outside world. This isolation is carried out by but is not limited to:

- **A Layer 3 device** using an Access List for restricting the specific type of traffic on any of its interfaces
- **A Layer 2 device** using the concept of VLANs or Private VLANs (PVLAN) for separating the traffic of two or more networks
- **A dedicated host device** with the installed software. This host device, which also serves as a proxy, filters the traffic that is desired while allowing the rest to pass through.

Firewall Architecture

Bastion Host

A Bastion Host is a computer system placed between public and private networks. It is intended to be a crossing point through which traffic passes. The system is assigned certain roles and responsibilities. Bastion host has two interfaces, one connected to the public network and the other to a private network.

Screened Subnet

A firewall with three interfaces can be used to create a screened subnet. The internal Private Network, Public Network, and Demilitarized Zone are connected through these three interfaces (DMZ). Each zone is segregated from the others in this architecture, so any compromise in one will not affect the others.

Multi-homed Firewall

A Multi-homed Firewall is two or more networks where each interface is connected to its network. It increases the efficiency and reliability of a network. A firewall with two or more interfaces allows further subdivision.

Demilitarized Zone (DMZ)

In contexts where security is done via routers, an IOS zone-based firewall is a set of rules that can mitigate mid-level security assaults. Device interfaces are deployed in separate unique zones (inside, outside, or DMZ) in Zone-based Firewalls (ZBF), and then policies are implemented to these zones. Zone naming guidelines must be simple to comprehend to be useful during troubleshooting.

Types of Firewall

Packet Filtering Firewall

Access lists are used in a Packet Filtering Firewall to permit or prohibit traffic depending on layer 3 and layer 4 information. When a packet arrives at the interface of an ACL-configured layer 3 devices, it checks for a match in the ACL (starting from the first line of ACL). Using an extended ACL in the Cisco device, the following information can be used to match traffic:

- Source Address
- Destination Address
- Source Port
- Destination Port
- Some extra features like TCP established sessions

Circuit-level Gateway Firewall

A Circuit-level Gateway Firewall operates at the session layer of the OSI model. It captures the packet to monitor the TCP Handshake in order to validate whether the sessions are legitimate. Packets forwarded to the remote destination through a circuit-level firewall appear to be originated from the gateway.

Application-level Firewall

An Application-level Firewall can work at layer 3 up to layer 7 of the OSI model. Normally, a specialized or open-source software running on a high-end server acts as an intermediary between client and destination address. As these firewalls can operate up to layer 7, it is possible to control moving in and out of more granular packets. Similarly, because the connection request stops on Application/Proxy firewalls, it becomes extremely difficult for an attacker to obtain a topological view of a trusted network.

Stateful Multilayer Inspection-based Firewalls

As the name implies, this saves the status of current sessions in a table known as a stateful database. Stateful inspection and firewalls that use it often block all traffic between trusted and untrusted interfaces. Whenever an end-device from a trusted interface wants to communicate with some destination address attached to the untrusted interface of the firewall, it will be entered in a stateful database table containing layer 3 and layer 2 information. The following table compares different features of stateful inspection-based firewalls.

Transparent Firewalls

The majority of the firewalls mentioned above operate at layer 3 and beyond. Transparent firewalls work in the same way as the strategies listed above, but the firewall's interfaces are layer 2 in nature. There are no IP addresses assigned to any interfaces - imagine a switch with ports assigned to a VLAN. The transparent firewall has only one IP address given to it for administration purposes. Similarly, as there is no extra hop between end devices, the user will not be aware of any new additions to the network infrastructure, and custom-made applications may work without any problem.

Next Generation (NGFW) Firewalls

NGFW is a relatively new term used for the latest firewalls with advanced feature sets. This kind of firewall provides in-depth security features to mitigate known threats and malware attacks. An example of next-generation firewalls is the Cisco ASA series with FirePOWER services. NGFW provides complete visibility into network traffic users, mobile devices, Virtual Machines (VM) to VM data communication, etc.

Personal Firewalls

A Personal Firewall is also known as a desktop firewall. It helps to protect end-users personal computers from general attacks from intruders. Such firewalls appear to be a great security line of defense for users who are constantly connected to the internet via DSL or cable modem. Personal firewalls help by providing inbound and outbound filtering, controlling internet connectivity to and from the computer (both in a domain-based and workgroup mode), and alerting the user of any intrusion attempts.

Honeypot

Honeypots are devices or systems deployed to trap attackers attempting to gain unauthorized access to a system or network. They are deployed in an isolated environment and are monitored. Typically, honeypots are deployed in DMZ and configured identically to a server. Any probe, malware, or infection will be immediately detected as the honeypot appears to be a legitimate part of the network.

IDS, Firewall, and Honeypot System

Snort

Snort is an open-source intrusion prevention system that delivers the most effective and comprehensive real-time network defense solutions. Snort is capable of protocol analysis, real-time packet analysis, and logging. It can also search and filter content and detect various attacks and probes, including buffer overflows, port scans, SMB probes, and much more. Snort can also be used in various forms, including a packet sniffer, a packet logger, a network file logging device, or a full-blown network intrusion prevention system.

Snort Rule

Rules are a criterion for performing detection against threats and vulnerabilities to the system and network, which leads to the advantage of zero-day attack detection. Unlike signatures, rules focus on detecting actual vulnerabilities. There are two ways to get Snort Rules:

1. Snort Subscriber Rule
2. Snort Community Rule

Categories of Snort Rules

There are different categories of Snort rule, and TALOS frequently updates these. Some of these categories are:

Application Detection Rule Category: includes the rules for monitoring and controlling the traffic of certain applications. These rules control the behavior and network activities of applications.

Black List Rules Category: includes the URL, IP address, DNS, and other rules determined as an indicator of malicious activities.

Browsers Category: includes the rule for detection of vulnerabilities in certain browsers.
- browser-chrome.rules
- browser-firefox.rules
- browser-ie.rules
- browser-webkit
- browser-other
- browser-plugins

Operating System Rules Category: includes rules looking for vulnerabilities in OS.
- os-Solaris
- os-windows
- os-mobile
- os-Linux
- os-other

Evading IDS

Insertion Attack

An Insertion Attack is a kind of evasion of an IDS device done by taking advantage of users' blind belief in IDS. The Intrusion Detection System (IDS) assumes that the end systems also accept accepted packets, but there may be a possibility that the end system rejects these packets. This type of attack particularly targets Signature-based IDS devices to insert data into the IDS. An attacker can insert packets with bad checksum or TTL values and send them out of order by taking advantage of a vulnerability. The IDS and end host, when reassembling the packet, might have two different streams.

Evasion

Evasion is a technique for sending a packet through the IDS that is accepted by the end system but rejected by the IDS. The goal of evasion tactics is to take advantage of the host. An IDS that incorrectly rejects such a packet completely misses its contents. An adversary could take advantage of this situation and profit from it.

Fragmentation Attack

Fragmentation is the process of splitting a packet into fragments. This technique is usually adopted when the IDS and host device are configured with different timeouts. For example, if IDS is configured with 10 seconds of timeout while the host is configured with 20 seconds of the timeout, sending packets with a 15-second delay will bypass reassembly at IDS and reassemble at the host.

Denial-of-Service Attack (DoS)

Passive IDS devices are inherently Fail-Open rather than Fail-Closed. An attacker may launch a denial-of-service attack on the network to overload the IDS System by taking advantage of this limitation. To perform a DoS attack on IDS, an attacker may target CPU exhaustion or Memory Exhaustion techniques to overload the IDS. These can be done by sending specially crafted packets consuming more CPU resources or sending many fragmented out-of-order packets.

Obfuscating

Obfuscation is the encryption of a packet's payload destined to a target in such a way that the target host can reverse it, but the IDS cannot. It exploits the end-user without alerting the IDS, using a different encoding, encryption, and polymorphism techniques. The IDS does not inspect encrypted protocols unless configured with the server's private key to encrypt the packets. Similarly, an attacker may use polymorphic shellcode to create unique patterns to evade IDS.

False Positive Generation

False Positive Alert Generation is the false indication of a result inspected for a particular condition or policy. An attacker may generate many false-positive alerts by sending a suspicious packet containing real malicious packets to pass the IDS.

Session Splicing

Session Splicing is a technique in which an attacker splits the traffic into a large number of the smaller packets in a way that not even a single packet triggers the alert. This can also be done by a slightly different technique, such as adding a delay between packets. This technique is effective for those IDS that do not reassemble the sequence to check against intrusion.

Unicode Evasion Technique

The Unicode Evasion Technique is another technique in which an attacker may use Unicode to manipulate the IDS. Unicode is a character encoding, as defined earlier in the HTML Encoding section. Converting strings using Unicode characters can prevent signature matching and alerting the IDS, thus bypassing the detection system.

Evading Firewalls

Firewall Identification

Identification of firewalls includes firewall fingerprinting to obtain sensitive information such as open ports, the version of services running in a network, etc. This information is extracted using different techniques, for example, Port Scanning, Fire-Walking, Banner Grabbing, etc.

Port Scanning

Port Scanning is an examination procedure mostly used by attackers to identify the open port. However, legitimate users may also use it. Port scanning does not always lead to an attack, as the user and attacker use it. However, it is a network reconnaissance that can be used to collect information before an attack. In this scenario, special packets are forwarded to a particular host whose response is examined by the attacker to get information regarding open ports.

Firewalking

Firewalking is a technique in which an attacker, using an ICMP packet, finds out the location of the firewall and networking map by probing the ICMP echo request with TTL values incrementing one by one. It helps the attacker to find out the number of hops.

Banner Grabbing

Banner Grabbing is another technique in which information from a banner is grabbed. Different devices such as routers, firewalls, and web servers display a banner in the console after login in through FTP or Telnet. Using banner grabbing, an attacker can extract the target device's vendor information and firmware version information.

IP Address Spoofing

Spoofing an IP address to obtain unwanted access to a machine is known as IP address spoofing. An attacker can illegally mimic any user machine by delivering altered IP packets with a faked IP address. The spoofing method comprises adding a spoofed source IP address, a checksum, and order values to the header.

Source Routing

Source Routing is the technique of sending a packet via a selected route. In session hijacking, this technique is used to attempt IP spoofing as a legitimate host, and with the help of source routing, the traffic is directed through a path identical to the victim's path.

IDS/Firewall Evasion Countermeasures

It is difficult to manage and prevent an evasion method. However, there are several tactics that can make it difficult for an attacker to go undetected. These defensive and monitoring strategies ensure that the detection system secures the network while also allowing for better traffic control. These techniques are for basic troubleshooting and monitoring, while others are for correct IPS/IDS and firewall settings. Initially observe and debug the firewall by:

- Port scanning
- Banner grabbing
- Firewalking
- IP address spoofing
- Source routing
- Bypassing firewall using IP in URL
- Attempting a fragmentation attack
- Troubleshooting behavior using proxy servers
- Troubleshooting behavior using ICMP tunneling

Chapter 13: Hacking Web Servers

Technology Brief
Web Servers are programs that are used for hosting websites. Web servers can be deployed on separate web server hardware or installed on a host as a program. The use of web applications has increased over the last few years. New web applications are flexible and capable of supporting larger clients. This chapter will discuss web server vulnerabilities, techniques and tools for attacking them, and mitigation methods.

Web Server Concepts
A Web Server is a program that hosts websites based on both hardware and software. It delivers files and other content on the website over HyperText Transfer Protocol (HTTP). As the use of the internet and intranet has increased, web services have become a major part of the internet. They are used for delivering files, email communication, and other purposes. Whereas all web servers support HTML for basic content delivery, they support different types of application extensions. Web servers differ regarding security models, Operating Systems, and other factors.

Web Server Security Issues
Security Issues for web servers may include network-level attacks and Operating System-level attacks. Usually, an attacker will target any vulnerability or error in web server configuration and exploit these loopholes. These vulnerabilities may include:

- Improper permission of file directories
- Default configuration
- Enabling unnecessary services
- Lack of security
- Bugs
- Misconfigured SSL Certificates
- Enabling debugging

Open Source Web Server Architecture
Open Source Web Server Architecture is the webserver model in which an open-source web server is hosted, either on a web server or a third-party host over the internet. The most popular and widely-used open source web servers are:

- Apache HTTP Server
- NGINX
- Apache Tomcat
- Lighttpd
- Node.js

IIS Web Server Architecture
Internet Information Services (IIS) is a Windows-based service that provides a request processing architecture. IIS's latest version is 7.x. The architecture includes Windows Process Activation Services (WAS), Web Server Engine, and Integrated Request Processing Pipelines. IIS contains multiple components responsible for several functions such as listening to a request, managing processes, reading configuration files, etc.

Components of IIS
Components of IIS include:

- Protocol Listeners
- HTTP.sys
- World Wide Web Publishing Service (WWW Service)
- Windows Process Activation Service (WAS)

Web Server Attacks
There are several Web Server Attacking techniques, some of which were defined earlier in this workbook. The remaining techniques are defined below:

DoS/DDoS Attacks
DOS/DDOS attacks flood fake requests towards the web server resulting in crashing, unavailability, or denial of service for all users.

DNS Server Hijacking
By compromising the DNS server, an attacker modifies the DNS configuration. Modification results in redirecting requests meant for the target webserver to the malicious server owned or controlled by the attacker.

DNS Amplification Attack

A DNS Amplification Attack is performed with the help of the DNS recursive method. An attacker takes advantage of this feature and spoofs the lookup request to the DNS server. The DNS server sends the request to the spoofed address, i.e., the address of the target. Amplifying the size of the request and using botnets result in a distributed denial-of-service attack.

Directory Traversal Attacks

In this type of attack, attackers use the trial and error method to access restricted directories using dots and slash sequences. By accessing the directories outside the root directory, attackers can reveal sensitive information about the system.

Man-in-the-Middle/Sniffing Attack

As defined in previous chapters, using a Man-in-the-Middle Attack, an attacker places him/herself between the client and server and sniffs the packets. He/she extracts sensitive information from the communication by intercepting and altering the packets.

Phishing Attacks

By using Phishing Attacks, an attacker attempts to extract login details from a fake website that appears to be a legitimate website. The attacker tries to impersonate a legitimate user on the actual target server, using stolen information, usually credentials.

Website Defacement

Website Defacement is a process in which attackers, after successful intrusion into a legitimate website, alter, modify, and change the appearance of the website. Accessing and defacing a website can be performed with several techniques, such as SQL injection.

Web Server Misconfiguration

Another method of attack is finding vulnerabilities in a website and exploiting them. An attacker may look for misconfigurations and vulnerabilities in the system and web server components. The attacker may identify weaknesses in terms of the default configuration, remote functioning, misconfigurations, default certification, and debug in order to exploit them.

HTTP Response Splitting Attack

HTTP Response Splitting Attacks are techniques in which an attacker sends response-splitting requests to the server. In this way, an attacker can add a header response, resulting in the server splitting the response into two. The second response comes under the attacker's control so the user can be redirected to the malicious website.

Web Cache Poisoning Attack

A Web Cache Poisoning Attack is a technique in which an attacker wipes the actual cache of the web server and stores fake entries by sending a crafted request into the cache. This will redirect the users to malicious web pages.

SSH Brute-Force Attack

Brute-Forcing the SSH tunnel allows an attacker to use an encrypted tunnel. This encrypted tunnel is used for communication between hosts. By brute-forcing the SSH login credentials, an attacker can gain unauthorized access to the SSH tunnel.

Web Application Attacks

Other web application related attacks include:

- Cookie Tampering
- DoS Attack
- SQL Injection
- Session Hijacking
- Cross-Site Request Forgery (CSRF) Attack
- Cross-Site Scripting (XSS) Attack
- Buffer overflow

Attack Methodology

Information Gathering

Information gathering involves collecting information about a target using different platforms, either through social engineering or internet surfing. An attacker may use different tools and networking commands to extract information. They may also navigate to the robot.txt file to extract information about internal files.

Web Server Footprinting

This includes footprinting focused on the webserver using different tools such as Netcraft, Maltego, and httprecon, etc. The results of web server footprinting can include the server name, type, Operating System, running application, and other information about the target website.

Vulnerability Scanning

Vulnerability Scanners are automated utilities that scan an Operating System, network, software, and applications for vulnerabilities, flaws, faults, and holes. Scripts, open ports, banners, running services, configuration issues, and other areas are thoroughly examined by these scanning programs.

Session Hijacking

Session Hijacking is also known as TCP Session Hijacking. It is a technique for taking control of a user's web session by manipulating the session ID. The attacker steals a legitimate user's authenticated session without initiating a new session with the target server.

Hacking Web Passwords

Password Cracking is the method of extracting a password to gain authorized access to a target system in the guise of a legitimate user. Password cracking may be performed through a social engineering attack or cracking through tempering the communication and stealing the stored information.

Password attacks are classified as the following:

- Non-Electronic Attacks
- Active Online Attacks
- Passive Online Attacks
- Default Password
- Offline Attack

Countermeasures

The basic recommendation for securing a web server from internal and external attacks and other threats is to place the web server in a secure zone where security devices such as firewalls, IPS, and IDS are deployed to constantly filter and inspect the traffic destined to the webserver. Placing the webserver in an isolated environment such as a DMZ protects it from threats.

Chapter 14: Hacking Web Applications

Web Application Concepts

Web Applications run on a remote application server and are available for clients over the internet. A web application can be available on different platforms, for example, browsers and software. The use of web applications has increased enormously in the last few years. They are dependent on a Client-Server relationship and provide an interface to clients to use web services. Web pages may be generated on the server or might contain scripts for dynamic execution on the client web browser.

Server Administrator

The Server Administrator takes care of the safety, security, functionality, and performance of the webserver. It is responsible for estimating security measures, deploying security models, and finding and eliminating vulnerabilities.

Application Administrator

The web application's management and setup are the responsibility of the Application Administrator. It ensures the web application's availability and good performance.

Client

Clients are those endpoints that interact with the web server or application server to make use of the services offered by the server. These clients require a highly available service from the server at any given time. When the clients access the resources, they use various web browsers that might be risky in terms of security.

Web 2.0

Web 2.0 is the World Wide Web website generation that provides dynamic and flexible user interaction. It provides ease of use and interoperability between other products, systems, and devices. Web 2.0 allows users to interact and collaborate with social platforms such as social media and social networking sites. The previous version, known as web 1.0, was restricted to passively reading static material. Almost every user on Web 2.0 has the same ability to participate. Web 2.0 has a lot of user interaction and engagement and dynamic content, metadata, web standards, and scalability.

Web App Threats

Threats to Web Application include:

- Cookie Poisoning
- Insecure Storage
- Information Leakage
- Directory Traversal
- Parameter/Form Tampering
- DOS Attack
- Buffer Overflow
- Log Tampering
- SQL Injection
- Cross-Site (XSS)
- Cross-Site Request Forgery
- Security Misconfiguration
- Broken Session Management
- DMZ Attacks
- Session Hijacking
- Network Access Attacks

Web App Hacking Methodology

- Footprint Web Infrastructure
- Analyze Web Applications
- By-pass Client-side Control
- Attack Authentication Mechanism
- Authorization Attack Schemes
- Attack Access Control
- Session Management AttackPerform Injection Attacks
- Attack Database Connectivity
- Attack Web Client
- Attack Web Services
- Web APIs, WebHooks, & Web Shell

Secure Application Development and Deployment

Development of Life Cycle Models

Software production results from processes that involve requirements gathering, planning, designing, coding, testing, and supporting. These tasks are performed according to the process model enabled by the team members.

Waterfall Model

One of the frameworks of application development is the Waterfall Model, which is a "sequential design process". In this process, each step is taken sequentially; that is, the second step follows the completion of the first, the third step follows the completion of the second, and so forth.

Agile Model

In the Agile Model, no sequential path is followed. Instead, multiple tasks are performed simultaneously in development. An advantage of the Agile model is that making changes is easy, i.e., the development process in the Agile model is continuous.

The two major forms of Agile development are as follows:

- Scrum
- Extreme Programming (XP)

Secure DevOps

Security Automation

Automation is the key element of DevOps, and it relies on automation for most of its efficiencies. Security automation, as the name refers, automatically handles security-related tasks.

Continuous Integration

Continuous Integration (CI) in DevOps refers to the continuous upgrading and improvement of the production codebase. CI permits DevOps team members to update and test minor changes without much overhead through high-level automation and safety nets.

Baselining

Standardizing performance and functionality at a certain level is known as Baselining. This provides a reference point when changes are made, so it is so important to DevOps and security. Reference points are used to represent the improvements with each change. At the time of a major change or development, it is important for the development team to baseline the system.

Immutable System

A system that is never patched or upgraded once it is deployed is known as an Immutable System. If upgrading is needed, the system is simply replaced with a new patched or upgraded system. In a typical system (changeable system), it is difficult to perform authorized software and system updates and lockdown directories simultaneously. This is because updating the system creates temporary files in the directories and these directories contain some files that should never be modified. The immutable system resolves this problem.

Infrastructure as Code

Infrastructure as Code, or programmable infrastructure, refers to the usage of code to build a system, although a normal configuration mechanism is used to manually configure the code.

Infrastructure as code is a way of using automation to build out a reproducible and efficient system. It is considered a key attribute of enabling the best practices in DevOps.

Version Control and Change Management

Changes like bug fixes, security patches, new features, etc., in an application are guaranteed by the vendor. During the application development process, multiple changes need to be implemented, and that requires version control.

Version Control

Version Control tracks changes and can also revert back to see what changes have been made. This version control feature is used in multiple software and in the Operating System, cloud-based files, and wiki software. It is also important from a security perspective because it identifies required modifications with respect to time.

Provisioning and De-Provisioning

Provisioning refers to "making something available", for example, deploying an application. Necessary provisioning includes the web server, database server, certificate updates, user workstation configuration, etc.

De-provisioning is the process of removing an application. An important factor related to the de-provisioning of an application is that every instance of the application needs to be removed and verified.

Secure Coding Techniques

The Basic Concept of Secure Coding

The security of an application starts with code that is secure and free from any vulnerability. However, all codes have vulnerabilities and weaknesses. Thus, the goal is to create a code that maintains a desired level of security and possesses an effective defense against vulnerability exploitation.

If configuration, faults, and exceptions are handled properly, a secure application can be established. If an application is tested throughout the Software Development Life Cycle, the security risk profile of the system can be calculated (SDLC).

SDLM (Software Development Life Cycle Methodology) has components that can help with secure code development. The following are some SDLM processes that can help increase code security:

- Cross-Site Scripting
- Cross-Site Request Forgery
- Input Validation
- Error and Exceptional Handling

The most widely used source coding techniques include:

- Proper Error Handling
- Proper Input Validation
- Stored Procedure
- Code Signing
- Encryption
- Obfuscation
- Code Re-Use/ Dead Code
- Validation
- Memory Management
- Use of Third-Party Libraries and SDKs
- Data Exposure

Code Quality and Testing

Application developers use tools and techniques to assist them in testing and checking the security level of code. Code analysis is performed to find weaknesses and vulnerabilities. This analysis can be performed either dynamically or statically.

- Code Analysis
- Code Testing
- Static Code Analyzer
- Dynamic Analysis
- Stress Testing
- Sandboxing
- Model Verification

Verification

Verification is a process that checks whether the software is working properly, whether there are any bugs to address, or whether the product meets the model specifications.

Validation

Validation refers to the process of determining whether an application meets certain requirements, including high-level requirements, secure software building requirements, security requirements, and compatibility. It also investigates whether or not the product is right for an organization.

Compiled vs. Runtime Code

When the source code is compiled into an executable, it is called Compiled Code. Once the code is compiled, the source code becomes hidden (you do not see it). During the process of compilation, any bugs and errors that can be resolved by recompiling the code are identified by the compiler. After fixing the bugs, an error-free application can be developed.

An Overview of Federated Identities

Server-based Authentication

The process of Server-based Authentication is as follows:

1. When the client logs in to the session, information is received by the server.
2. The server checks the session information when the client sends an application request.
3. If the session information is authentic, the feedback is sent to the client.

Token-based Authentication

The process of token-based authentication is as follows:

1. The client logs in to the server.

2. After investigating the validity of the authentication process, a token is sent to the client.
3. The client sends that token along with the application request.
4. If the token is valid, the server responds to the client.

Federation

Federation is a system that grants access to other users who may not have local login. It means a single token is given to the user who is entrusted or authenticated across various systems, just like in SSO (Single Sign-On). A federated network is created by third parties so that users can log in with separate credentials, for example, Facebook credentials, Twitter credentials, etc. Before establishing a federated network, the third party has to create a trust-based relationship.

Security Assertion Mark-up Language (SAML)

SAML is an open standard authentication and authorization method. The user is authenticated for achieving entry to local sources through a third party. Shibboleth software is an example of SAML. It is a security concern that modern mobile networks do not have SAML support.

OAuth

This was introduced by Google, Twitter, and other parties. It acts as permission to the resources that a user has access to. Facebook, Google, and other companies commonly employ OAuth. It is not an authentication protocol but rather one that allows programs to communicate with one another. After combining OAuth with OpenID Connect (which handles SSO), OAuth determines which resources a user has access to.

Important Considerations for Best Practices

Encoding Schemes

Web applications use different encoding schemes for securing their data. There are two categories of the encoding scheme.

URL Encoding

URL encoding is a method of encoding that allows a URL to be securely handled. The URL is transformed to ASCII representation for secure transmission over HTTP during URL encoding. Unusual ASCII characters are replaced with ASCII code, and a "%" is followed by two hexadecimal digits.

Chapter 15: SQL Injection

SQL Injection Concepts

SQL Injection Attacks target websites or web applications that employ SQL databases. It works by injecting harmful code or scripts into current queries strategically. This malicious code is written to expose or modify data housed in a database's tables.

SQL injection is a very hazardous and strong attack. It detects and reports faults and vulnerabilities in a website or application. The basic idea behind SQL injection is to inject commands into a database to divulge sensitive data. As a result, a high-profile attack is possible.

The Scope of SQL Injection

SQL Injection can be a serious threat to a website or application. The impact of an SQL injection can be measured by observing the following parameters that an attacker attempts to affect:

- Bypassing Authentication
- Revealing Sensitive Information
- Compromising Data integrity
- Erasing the Database
- Remote Code Execution

Types of SQL Injection

SQL injection is classified into three major categories:

1. In-band SQLi
2. Inferential SQLi
3. Out-of-band SQLi

In-band SQL Injection

In-band SQL Injection refers to injection techniques that use the same communication channel to launch an attack and collect data from the response. Techniques for in-band injection include:

1. Error-based SQL Injection
2. Union-based SQL Injection

Error-based SQL Injection

Error-based SQL Injection is an in-band SQL injection technique. It relies on error messages from the database server to reveal information about the structure of the database. Error-based SQL injection is very useful for an attacker to enumerate an entire database. Error messages are used during the development phase to troubleshoot issues. These messages should be disabled when an application website is live. Error-based SQL injection can be performed using the following techniques:

- System Stored Procedure
- End of Line Comment
- Illegal/Logically incorrect Query
- Tautology

Union SQL Injection

Union-based SQL Injection is another in-band SQL injection technique that involves using the UNION SQL operator to combine the results of two or more SELECT statements into a single result.

Inferential SQL Injection (Blind Injection)

In an Inferential SQL Injection, no data is transferred from a web application. These are referred to as Blind Injections because the attacker cannot see the results of an attack; he/she simply observes the server's behavior. The two types of inferential SQL injection are Boolean-based Blind SQL Injection and Time-based Blind SQL Injection.

Boolean Exploitation Technique

Blind SQL injection is the technique of sending a request to a database. As the response is either true or false, it does not contain any database data. By observing the HTTP response, the attacker can evaluate it and infer whether the injection was successful or unsuccessful.

Out-of-band SQL Injection

Out-of-band SQL Injection is a technique that uses different channels to launch the injection and to gather the response. It requires some features to be enabled, for example, DNS or HTTP requests on the database server; hence, it is not very common.

SQL Injection Methodology

Information Gathering and SQL Injection Vulnerability Detection

In the Information Gathering phase, information about the web application, Operating System, database, and the structure of the components is collected. Evaluation of the extracted information is useful for identifying vulnerabilities that can be exploited. Information can be gathered by using different tools and techniques, such as injecting code into the input fields to observe the response of error messages. Evaluation of the input fields, hidden fields, get and post requests, cookies, string values, and detailed error messages can reveal enough information to initiate an injection attack.

Advanced SQL Injection

Advanced SQL injection may include an enumeration of databases such as MySQL, MSSQL, MS Access, Oracle, DB2, or Postgre SQL, tables and columns to identify users' privilege levels and account information of the database administrator, and database structure disclosure. It can also include password and hash grabbing and transferring the database to a remote machine.

Evasion Techniques

To secure a database, it is recommended that deployment is isolated in a secure network location with an Intrusion Detection System (IDS). IDS continually monitors the network and host traffic as well as database applications. The attacker has to evade IDS to access the database using different evasion techniques. For example, IDS using the Signature-based Detection System compares the input strings against the signature to detect intrusion. Now, all an attacker has to do is evade signature-based detection.

Types of Signature Evasion Techniques

The techniques below are used for evasion:

- Inserting Inline Comments between Keywords
- Character Encoding
- String Concatenating
- Obfuscating Codes
- Manipulating White Spaces
- Hex Encoding
- Sophisticated Matches

Countermeasures

Several detection tools are available to mitigate SQL injection attacks. These tools test websites and applications, report the data and issues and take remediation action. Some of these advanced tools also offer a technical description of the issue.

Chapter 16: Hacking Wireless Networks

Wireless Network Concepts

The wireless network is a computer network capable of transmitting and receiving data through a wireless medium such as radio waves. The major advantage of this type of network is the reduced costs of wires and devices, etc., and the ease of installation compared to the complexity of wired networks. Usually, wireless communication relies on radio communication. Different frequency ranges are used for different types of wireless technology depending on requirements. The most common wireless networks are cell phone networks, satellite communications, microwave communications, etc. These wireless networks are popularly used for Personal, Local, Wide Area Networks.

Wireless Network Terminologies

Global System for Mobile Communication (GSM)

The European Telecommunication Standards Institute (ETSI) established the Global System for Mobile Communication (GSM) as a standard. It is a digital cellular network's second-generation (2G) protocol. The 2G technology was created to replace the 1G (analog) technology. The 2G standard has been replaced by the 3G UMTS standard, which the 4G LTE standard will follow. Most GSM networks use the 900 MHz and 1800 MHz frequency bands.

Wireless Access Point (WAP)

An Access Point (AP) or Wireless Access Point (WAP) in a wireless network is a hardware device that provides wireless communication to end devices. The access point can be integrated with a router or attached to the router as a standalone device.

Service Set Identifier (SSID)

The name of an access point is called the Service Set Identifier (SSID). In technical terms, an SSID is a 32-bit token used to identify 802.11 networks (Wi-Fi). The SSID of the Wi-Fi network is broadcast continually (if enabled). This broadcasting serves as a means of identifying yourself and gaining access to the wireless network. Wireless devices will not detect the wireless network if the SSID broadcast is off unless each device is individually set with the SSID. To avoid compromise, default parameters such as the default SSID and password must be modified.

Basic Service Set Identifier (BSSID)

The service set consists of a group of wireless devices within a network. Basic service is a sub-group within a service set, a 48-bit label that conforms to MAC-48 conventions. A device may have multiple BSSIDs. Usually, each BSSID is associated with at most one basic service set at a time.

ISM Band

The Industrial, Scientific, and Medical (ISM) band, sometimes known as the unlicensed band, is a radio frequency band designated for industrial, scientific, and medical purposes. ISM uses the 2.54 GHz frequency range exclusively. This band is used by microwave ovens, cordless phones, medical diathermy machines, military radars, and industrial heaters, among other things.

Types of Wireless Networks

The types of Wireless Networks deployed in a geographical area are categorized as:

- Wireless Personal Area Network (Wireless PAN)
- Wireless Local Area Network (WLAN)
- Wireless Metropolitan Area Network (WMAN)
- Wireless Wide Area Network (WWAN)

Wi-Fi Technology

Wi-Fi is wireless local area networking technology that follows 802.11 standards. Many devices such as personal computers, gaming consoles, mobile phones, tablets, modern printers, and many more are Wi-Fi compatible. These Wi-Fi Compatible devices are connected to the internet through a Wireless Access Point. Several sub-protocols in 802.11, such as 802.11 a/b/g/n, are used in WLAN.

Wi-Fi Authentication Modes

There are two basic modes of authentication in Wi-Fi-based networks:

1. Open Authentication
2. Shared Key Authentication

Wi-Fi Authentication with Centralized Authentication Server

Nowadays, the basic WLAN technology most commonly and widely deployed worldwide is IEEE 802.11. The authentication option for the IEEE 802.11 network is the **Shared-Key-Authentication** mechanism or **WEP** (Wired Equivalency Privacy). Another option is **Open Authentication**. These options cannot secure the wireless network; hence, IEEE 802.11 to date remains insecure.

Wi-Fi Chalking

Wi-Fi Chalking includes several methods of detecting open wireless networks. These techniques include:

- **War Walking:** Walking around to detect open Wi-Fi networks
- **War Chalking:** Using symbols and signs to advertise open Wi-Fi networks
- **War Flying:** Detection of open Wi-Fi networks using drones
- **WarDriving:** Driving around to detect open Wi-Fi networks

Types of Wireless Antenna

Directional Antenna

Directional Antennas are antennas designed to operate in a specified direction to improve antenna efficiency and communication by eliminating interference. A dish commonly used for satellite TV and the internet is the most common type of directional antenna. Yagi antennas, quad antennas, horn antennas, billboard antennas, and helical antennas are directional antennas.

Omnidirectional Antenna

Omnidirectional Antennas radiate uniformly in all directions. The radiation pattern is often described as Doughnut shaped. The most common use of an omnidirectional antenna is radio broadcasting, cell phones, and GPS. Types of omnidirectional antennas include Dipole Antenna and Rubber Ducky Antenna.

Parabolic Antenna

Parabolic Antenna, as the name suggests, depends on a parabolic reflector. The curved surface of the parabola directs the radio waves. The most popular type of parabolic antenna is called Dish Antenna or Parabolic Dish. These are commonly used in radars, weather detection, satellite television, etc.

Yagi Antenna

Yagi-Uda Antenna, commonly known as Yagi antenna, is a directional antenna comprised of parasitic elements and driven elements. It is lightweight, inexpensive, and simple to construct. It is used in terrestrial television and point-to-point fixed radar communication, etc.

Dipole Antenna

The dipole antenna is the simplest antenna consisting of two identical dipoles. One side is connected to the feed line, whereas another is connected to the ground. The most popular use of a dipole antenna is in FM reception and TV.

Wireless Encryption

WEP Encryption

Wired Equivalent Privacy (WEP) is the oldest and weakest encryption protocol. It was developed to ensure the security of wireless protocols. However, it is highly vulnerable. It uses 24-bit Initialization Vector (IV) to create a stream cipher RC4 with Cyclic Redundant Check (CRC) to ensure confidentiality and integrity. A standard 64-bit WEP uses a 40-bit key, 128-bit WEP uses a 104-bit key, and 256-bit WEP uses a 232-bit key. Authentications used with WEP are Open System Authentication and Shared Key Authentication.

Weak Initialization Vectors (IV)

One of the major issues with WEP is with Initialization Vector (IV). The IV value is too small to protect from reuse and replay. The RC4 Algorithm uses IV and Key to create a stream using a Key Scheduling algorithm. Weak IV reveals information. WEP has no built-in provision to update the key.

Breaking WEP Encryption

Breaking WEP Encryption can be performed by following the steps outlined below:

1. Monitor the access point channel.

2. Test the injection capability of the access point.
3. Use tools to exploit authentication.
4. Sniff the packets using Wi-Fi sniffing tools.
5. Use an encryption tool to inject encrypted packets.
6. Use the cracking tool to extract the encryption key from IV.

WPA Encryption

Wi-Fi Protected Access (WPA) is another data encryption technique popularly used for WLAN networks based on 802.11i standards. This security protocol was developed by Wi-Fi Alliance to secure the WLAN networks against weaknesses and vulnerabilities found in Wired Equivalent Privacy (WEP). The deployment of WPA requires firmware upgrades for wireless network interface cards designed for WEP. Temporal Key Integrity Protocol (TKIP) dynamically generates a new key for each packet of 128-bits to prevent a threat that is vulnerable to WEP. WPA also contains a Message Integrity Check as a solution to Cyclic Redundancy Check (CRC) that was introduced to WEP to overcome the flaw of strong integrity validation.

Temporal Key Integrity Protocol

Temporal Key Integrity Protocol (TKIP) is used in IEEE 802.11i Wireless networks. This protocol is used in Wi-Fi Protected Access (WPA). TKIP has introduced three security features:

1. Secret root key and Initialization Vector (IV) Mixing before RC4.
2. Sequence Counter to ensure receiving in order and prevent replay attacks.
3. 64-bit Message Integrity Check (MIC).

WPA2 Encryption

WPA2 is intended to replace WPA by providing improved security using 192-bit encryption and specific encryption for each user, making it more difficult to hack. It employs encryption based on the Counter Mode Cipher Block Chaining Message Authentication Code Protocol (CCMP) and the Advanced Encryption Standard (AES). In 2018, Wi-Fi Allowance introduced WPA3, a more powerful security protocol that outperforms WPA2 functionality and security.

Wireless Threats

Access Control Attacks

Wireless Access Control Attacks are attacked in which an attacker penetrates the wireless network by evading access control parameters, for example, by spoofing the MAC address, rogue access point, and misconfigurations, etc.

Integrity and Confidentiality Attacks

WEP injection, data frame injection, replay attacks, and bit flipping are examples of integrity threats. To intercept confidential information, confidentiality attacks involve traffic analysis, session hijacking, masquerade, cracking, MITM attacks, and so on.

Availability Attacks

Availability Attacks include flooding and denial-of-service attacks that prevent legitimate users from connecting or accessing the wireless network. Availability attacks can be carried out by authentication flooding, ARP poisoning, de-authentication attacks, disassociation attack, etc.

Authentication Attacks

An Authentication Attack attempts to steal identified information or legitimated wireless client in order to gain access to the network by impersonating a legitimate user. It may include password cracking techniques, identity theft, password guessing.

Rogue Access Point Attack

A Rogue Access Point Attack is a technique whereby a legitimate wireless network is replaced with a rogue access point, usually with the same SSID. The user assumes the rogue access point as the legitimate access point and connects to it. Once a user is connected to the rogue access point, all traffic will direct through it, and the attacker can sniff the packet to monitor activity.

Client Misassociation

Client Misassociation includes a rogue access point outside the parameters of a corporate network. Once an employee is mistakenly connected to this rogue access point, all traffic will pass to the internet through the attacker.

Misconfigured Access Point Attack

A Misconfigured Access Point Attack gains access to a legitimate access point by taking benefit of its misconfigurations. A weak password, default password configuration, or a wireless network without password security, for example, are all examples of misconfigurations.

Unauthorized Association
Unauthorized Association is another technique in which infected users act as an access point, allowing an attacker to connect to the corporate network. These Trojans create a soft access point through malicious scripting, allowing devices such as laptops to turn their WLAN cards into transmitters, transmitting the WLAN network.

Ad Hoc Connection Attack
Ad Hoc Connection is an insecure network because it does not provide strong authentication and encryption. An attacker may attempt to compromise the client in ad hoc mode.

Signal Jamming Attack
A Signal-Jamming Attack requires high gain frequency signals, which cause a denial-of-service attack. The Carrier Sense Multiple Access/Collision Avoidance Algorithm requires waiting time to transmit after detecting a collision.

Wireless Hacking Methodology

Wi-Fi Discovery
Obtaining knowledge about a wireless network is the first step in hacking it to compromise it. Active and passive footprinting and the use of other tools can be used to collect data. Passive footprinting includes sniffing packets using tools such as Airwaves, Net Surveyor, and others to reveal information such as which live wireless networks are around. Active footprinting includes probing the access point to obtain information. In active footprinting, the attacker sends a probe request, and the access point sends a probe response.

GPS Mapping
GPS mapping is the process of creating a list of Wi-Fi networks that have been found using GPS. The GPS traces the location of the Wi-Fi networks, and this information can then be sold to an attacker or hacking community.

Wireless Traffic Analysis
Traffic analysis of a wireless network includes capturing the packet to reveal any information such as broadcast SSID, authentication methods, encryption techniques, etc. There are several tools available to capture and analyze a wireless network, for example, Wireshark/Pilot tool, Omni peek, Commview, etc.

Launch Wireless Attacks
Attackers use tools, such as Aircrack-ng, and other attacks, such as ARP poisoning, MITM, Fragmentation, MAC Spoofing, De-authentication, Disassociation, and rogue access point, to initiate an attack on a wireless network.

Bluetooth Hacking
Attacks on Bluetooth-based communication are referred to as Bluetooth hacking. Bluetooth is a widely used wireless technology that may be found in practically all mobile devices. Bluetooth technology is used to communicate between devices across short distances. It uses the 2.4 GHz band and has a range of up to 10 meters.

Bluetooth Attacks
- Blue Smacking
- Bluebugging
- Blue Jacking
- Blue Printing
- Bluesnarfing

Wireless Intrusion Prevention Systems (WIPS)
The Wireless Intrusion Prevention System (WIPS) is a wireless network device. It keeps an eye on the wireless network, defends it from unwanted access points, and performs intrusion prevention automatically. Prevents rogue access points by monitoring the radio spectrum and sending alarms to the network administrator. The fingerprinting approach helps to avoid devices with spoofed MAC addresses. WIPS consists of three components, server, sensor, and console. Rogue access points misconfigured APs, client misconfiguration, MITM, ad hoc networks, MAC spoofing, Honeypots, DoS attacks can all be mitigated using WIPS.

Wi-Fi Security Auditing Tool
Using Wireless Security tools is another approach to protecting wireless networks. This security software provides wireless network auditing, troubleshooting, detection, intrusion prevention, threat mitigation, rogue detection, day-zero threat protection, forensic investigation, and compliance reporting. Some of the popular Wi-Fi security tools are as follows:

- AirMagnet WiFi Analyzer

- Motorola's AirDefense Services Platform (ADSP)
- Cisco Adaptive Wireless IPS
- Aruba RFProtect

Chapter 17: Hacking Mobile Applications

Mobile Platform Attack Vectors

OWASP Top 10 Mobile Threats

OWASP stands for Open Web Application Security Project. OWASP provides unbiased and practical information about computer and internet applications. According to OWASP, the top 10 mobile threats are:

- Improper Platform Usage
- Insecure Data Storage
- Insecure Communication
- Insecure Authentication
- Insufficient Cryptography
- Insecure Authorization
- Client Code Quality
- Code Tampering
- Reverse Engineering
- Extraneous Functionality

Mobile Attack Vector

There are several types of threats and attacks used on mobile devices. Some of the most basic threats are malware, data loss, and attacks on integrity. An attacker may launch attacks through a victim's browser using a malicious website or a compromised legitimate website. Social engineering attacks, data loss, data theft, data exfiltration are the most common attacks on mobile technology. The mobile attack vector includes:

- Malware
- Data Loss
- Data Tampering
- Data Exfiltration

Vulnerabilities and Risks on Mobiles

Apart from attacks, there are several other vulnerabilities and risks to a mobile platform. The most common risks are:

- Malicious third-party applications
- Malicious applications on Store
- Malware and rootkits
- Application vulnerability
- Data security
- Excessive permissions
- Weak encryptions
- Operating System update issues
- Application update issues
- Jailbreaking and Rooting
- Physical attack

Hacking Android OS

A popular feature of Android is its flexibility with third-party applications. Users can download, install, and remove these applications (APK) files from application stores or from the internet. However, because of the platform's open-source nature, this can be a security risk; any third-party application can violate the policy of a trusted application. Many Android hacking tools outlined in this workbook are also not available in the Play store.

Device Administration API

Android 2.2 introduces the Device Administration API. Device Administration API ensures system-level device administration and management over Android devices in a corporate network. Here are some examples of apps that could make use of the Device Administration API:

- Email clients
- Security applications that can do a remote wipe
- Device management services and applications

Root Access/Android Rooting

Rooting, also known as Root Access, is the process of gaining privileged control over a device. Rooting is the process of acquiring privileged access to an Android device, such as a smartphone, tablet, or another device, via a subsystem in the Android Operating System. As previously stated, Android is a modified version of the Linux kernel with "superuser" permissions granted via root access. Root access is necessary to change administrator-only settings and configurations; however,

It can be used to change system applications and settings to get around constraints and restrictions.

Android Phone Security Tools

On the Google Play store, you may discover various anti-virus, security, vulnerability scanning, anti-theft, and "find my phone" tool. These are some of the tools:

- DroidSheep Guard
- TrustGo Mobile Security
- Sophos Mobile Security
- 360 Security
- Avira Antivirus Security
- AVL
- X-ray

Hacking iOS

The Operating System Apple.Inc developed for iPhones is known as iOS. It is one of the most popular Operating Systems for mobile devices, including iPhones, iPads, and iPods. The user interface in iOS is based on direct manipulation using multi-touch gestures. Major iOS versions are released annually. The current version, iOS 14, was released in March 2021. iOS uses hardware-accelerated AES-256 encryption and other additional encryption to encrypt data. iOS also isolates the application from other applications. Applications are not allowed to access another app's data.

Jailbreaking iOS

Jailbreaking is the concept of breaking the restriction "Jail". Jailbreaking is a form of rooting resulting in privilege escalation. iOS jailbreaking is the process of escalating privileges on iOS devices to either remove or bypass the factory default restrictions on software by using kernel patches or device customization. Jailbreaking allows root access to an iOS device, allowing unofficial applications to be downloaded. Jailbreaking is used to remove limitations, install new software, introduce malware, and pirate software.

Types of Jailbreaking

BIOS jailbreaking is divided into three categories based on privilege levels, system vulnerabilities, first and third bootloader vulnerabilities, and so forth. Apple can patch using the iBoot and Userland exploits.

- Userland Exploit
- iBoot Exploit
- Bootrom Exploit

Jailbreaking Techniques

- Tethered Jailbreaking
- Semi-tethered Jailbreaking
- Untethered Jailbreaking

Hacking Windows Phone OS

Windows Phone (WP) is another Operating System in the OS family, developed by Microsoft. The first launch was Windows Phone 7. Windows 7.5 Mango, released later, has a very low hardware requirement of 800 MHz CPU and 256 MB Ram. Windows 7 devices are not capable of upgrading to Windows 8 due to hardware limitations. Windows 8, 8.1, released in 2014, is replaced by Windows 10, released in 2017.

Hacking BlackBerry

BlackBerry is another smartphone company that is formerly known as Research in Motion (RIM) Ltd. BlackBerry was considered the most prominent and secure mobile phone. Its Operating System is known as BlackBerry OS.

Mobile Device Management (MDM)

The basic purpose of implementing Mobile Device Management (MDM) is to deploy, maintain, and monitor mobile devices that make up the BYOD solution. Devices may include laptops, smartphones, tablets, notebooks, or any other electronic device that can be taken outside the corporate office, either home or to a public space, and then get connected to the corporate office. The following are some of the functions provided by MDM:

- Forcing a device to lock after certain login failures
- Enforcing a strong password policy on all BYOD devices
- Detecting any attempt to hack BYOD devices and then these devices' limiting network access
- Enforcing confidentiality by using encryption as per an organization's policy
- Administering and implementing Data Loss Prevention (DLP) for BYOD devices. This helps to prevent any kind of data loss due to an end user's carelessness

Mobile Security Guidelines

There are many techniques and methods that can be followed to avoid trouble while using mobile phones. Apart from built-in features and precautions, several tools are available on every official application store to provide a user with better security for their devices.

Chapter 18: IoT & OT Hacking

Introduction

This module is revised in CEHv11 with the objective of better understanding Operational Technology (OT) concepts and providing an overview of OT threats and attacks, OT hacking methodology, tools and techniques of OT hacking, and penetration testing.

Gartner defines OT as hardware and software that detects or causes a change by directly monitoring and/or controlling industrial equipment, assets, processes, and events.

Internet of Things (IoT) is an environment of physical devices, such as home appliances, electronic devices, sensors embedded in software programs, and network interface cards to make them capable of connecting and communicating with the network.

IoT Concept

IoT devices can use IoT gateways to communicate with the internet or communicate with the internet directly. The integration of controlled equipment, a logic controller, and advanced programmable electronic circuits makes them capable of communicating and being controlled remotely.

The architecture of IoT depends on five layers, as follows:

1. Application Layer
2. Middleware Layer
3. Internet Layer
4. Access Gateway Layer
5. Edge Technology Layer

IoT Communication Models

IoT devices can communicate with other devices in several ways. The following are some of the IoT communication models.

- Device-to-Device Model
- Device-to-Cloud Model
- Device-to-Gateway Model
- Back-end Data-sharing Model

Understanding IoT Attacks

The introduction of the Internet of Things (IoT) is fraught with difficulties. While it provides convenience, mobility, and greater control over operations, IoT technology also introduces dangers, weaknesses, and obstacles. The following are some of the significant issues that IoT technology faces:

1. Lack of Security
2. Vulnerable Interfaces
3. Physical Security Risk
4. Lack of Vendor Support
5. Difficulties Updating Firmware and OS
6. Interoperability Issues

IoT Attacks

DDoS Attack

A Distributed-Denial-of-Service Attack, as defined earlier, is intended to make the target's services unavailable. Using a Distributed-DOS attack, all IoT devices, IoT gateways, and application servers can be targeted, and flooding requests toward them can result in a denial of service.

Rolling Code Attack

Rolling Code or Code Hopping is another technique that can be exploited. In this technique, an attacker captures the code, sequence, or signal from transmitter devices while simultaneously blocking the receiver from receiving the signal. The captured code will later be used to gain unauthorized access.

BlueBorne Attack

The BlueBorne attack is performed using different techniques for exploiting Bluetooth vulnerabilities. These techniques used to gain unauthorized access to Bluetooth-enabled devices are called BlueBorne Attacks.

Jamming Attack

A Jamming Attack uses signals to prevent devices from communicating with each other and the server.

Backdoor

This involves deploying a Backdoor on an organization's computer to gain unauthorized access to the private network.

IoT Hacking Methodology

Hacking methodology for the IoT platform is the same as the methodology for other platforms.

Information Gathering

The first step in hacking the IoT environment requires information gathering. This includes extraction of information, such as IP address, running protocols, open ports, type of device, vendor information, etc. Shodan, Censys, and Thingful are search engines commonly used to find information about IoT devices.

Vulnerability Scanning

Vulnerability Scanning includes scanning networks and devices to identify weak passwords, software and firmware bugs, default configuration, etc. Multi-ping, Nmap, RIoT Vulnerability scanner, and Foren6 are used for scanning against vulnerabilities.

Launch Attack

The Launch Attack phase includes exploiting these vulnerabilities using different attacks like DDoS, Rolling Code, jamming, etc. RFCrack, Attify Zigbee Framework, and HackRF 1 are the most popular tools for launching attacks.

Gain Access

Gaining Access includes taking control of the IoT environment. This phase can also include gaining access, escalating privileges to the administrator, or installing a backdoor.

Maintain Attack

Maintaining an Attack includes logging out without being detected, clearing logs, and covering tracks.

Operational Technology (OT) Concept

Operational Technology is a broad term that covers the operational network of an organization, usually based on Industrial Control Systems (ICS). ICS refers to a control system based on devices, systems, and controls used for the operation or function of an automated industrial process. Different nature of industries utilizes different types of industrial controls having different functions with different protocols. ICS is used in almost every industrial sector, such as manufacturing, transportation, energy, aviation, and many more. There are various ICSs, with Supervisory Control and Data Acquisition (SCADA) systems and Distributed Control Systems being the most common (DCS).

OT Attacks

- 2017 Triton Malware Attack on Petrochemical Facilities | Middle East
- 2015 BlackEnergy Malware Attack on Ukrainian Power Grid

OT Hacking Methodology

Attacks on the IT-OT network require initial planning. Usually, sophisticated attacks are initiated by motivated threat actors to disrupt industrial processes. To fulfill their motives, they need to remain undetected for a long period of time, from intrusion till action on their objectives. ATT&CK for ICS is a knowledge base useful for describing an adversary's actions while operating within an ICS network. The knowledge base can be utilized to better classify and understand opponent conduct after a compromise has been reached.

1. **Initial Access** by compromising engineering workstation or drive-by-compromise
2. **Discovery** of control devices, modules, and services to intrude into OT network
3. **Inhibit Response Functions** such as alarm suppression, modification of control logic, denial of service, etc.
4. **Impair Process Control** by injecting malicious commands, parameter modification, etc.
5. **Impacts** such as denial of control, operational information theft, loss of safety, productivity, or revenue

Chapter 19: Cloud Computing

Introduction

Cloud Computing technology has gained popularity nowadays because of its flexibility and mobility support. Cloud computing allows access to personal and shared resources with minimal management. It often relies on the internet. There is also a third-party cloud solution available, which saves on expanding resources and maintenance. One popular example of cloud computing is Amazon Elastic Cloud Compute (EC2), which is highly capable, low cost, and flexible. The main features of cloud computing include:

- On-Demand Self-Service
- Distributed Storage
- Rapid Elasticity
- Measured Services
- Automated Management
- Virtualization

Types of Cloud Computing Services

There are three types of Cloud Computing Services:
- Infrastructure-as-a-Service (IaaS)
- Platform-as-a-Service (PaaS)
- Software-as-a-Service (SaaS)

Cloud Deployment Models

The following are the Deployment Models for cloud services:

- Public cloud
- Private cloud
- Hybrid cloud
- Community

Cloud Computing Benefits

There are abundant advantages of cloud computing, of which some of the most important are:
- Increased Capacity
- Increased Speed
- Low Latency
- Less Economic Expense
- Security

Understanding Virtualization

Virtualization in computer networking is the process of deploying a machine or multiple machines virtually on a host. These virtually deployed machines use the host machine's system resources by applying a logical division. The major difference between a physically deployed machine and a virtual machine is the system resources and hardware. Physical deployment requires separate dedicated hardware for a single Operating System, whereas a virtual machine host can support multiple Operating Systems over a single system, sharing resources such as storage.

Container Technology

Containers are defined by Google Cloud as "a conceptual packaging method that allows applications to be isolated from their real running environment. Regardless matter whether the target environment is a private datacenter, the public cloud, or even a developer's own laptop, this decoupling allows container-based apps to be deployed easily and consistently."

Virtual Machines and Containers are frequently compared (VM). Containers, like virtual machines, let you package your application with libraries and other dependencies, creating separate environments in which to operate your software services.

Serverless Computing

Serverless computing is another cloud computing service that provides backend services to the developers on a pay-as-you-go basis. The serverless computing model offers the development of agile applications where infrastructure management, capacity provisioning, and other tasks are handled by the service provider. Pay-as-you-go means the service provider will charge based on computation, eliminating the need for reservation, charges of a fixed amount of renting servers or bandwidth. The serverless model is auto-scalable and highly available. Although Serverless computing is cost-efficient, it could end up being very expensive in a DDoS attack scenario.

Cloud Computing Threats

Although cloud computing offers many services with efficiency and flexibility, there are also some threats from which cloud computing is vulnerable. These threats include data loss/breach, insecure interfaces and APIs, malicious insiders, privilege escalations, natural disasters, hardware failure, authentication problems, VM level attacks, and much more.

Data Loss/Breach

Data Loss and Data Breach are the most common threats to every platform. Improper encryption or loss of encryption keys may result in data modification, erasing, theft, or misuse.

Abusing Cloud Services

Abusing Cloud Services includes using the service for malicious intent as well as using these services abusively. For example, an attacker can abuse the Dropbox service by spreading a massive phishing campaign. Similarly, a cloud service can be used to host malicious data and botnet commands and controls, etc.

Insecure Interface and APIs

Software User Interface (UI) and Application Programming Interfaces (APIs) are the interfaces used by customers to interact with the service. They need to be secure from malicious attempts. Such interfaces can be made secure with good monitoring, orchestration, management, and provisioning program.

Cloud Computing Attacks

In cloud computing, the following are the most common attacks attackers use to extract sensitive information, such as personal credentials or gaining unauthorized access. Cloud Computing Attacks include:

- Service Hijacking with Social Engineering Attacks
- Session Hijacking with XSS Attacks
- Domain Name System (DNS) Attacks
- SQL Injection Attacks
- Wrapping Attacks
- Service Hijacking with Network Sniffing
- Session Hijacking with Session Riding
- Side Channel Attack or Cross-Guest VM Breaches
- Cryptanalysis
- DoS/DDoS Attacks

Cloud Security

Cloud Computing Security refers to the security implementation and deployment of a system to prevent security threats. Cloud security includes control policies, deployment of security devices such as application firewalls and Next-Generation IPS devices, and strengthening the cloud computing infrastructure. It also includes actions at the service provider end as well as the user end.

Cloud Security Control Layers

- Application Layer
- Information
- Management
- Network Layer
- Trusted Computing
- Computer and Storage
- Physical Security

Responsibilities in Cloud Security

Cloud Service Provider

The responsibilities of a cloud service provider include providing the following security controls:

- Web Application Firewall (WAF)
- Real Traffic Grabber (RTG)
- Firewall
- Data Loss Prevention (DLP)
- Intrusion Prevention Systems
- Secure Web Gateway (SWG)
- Application Security (App Sec)
- Virtual Private Network (VPN)
- Load Balancer
- CoS/QoS
- Trusted Platform Module
- Netflow and others

Cloud Service Consumer

The responsibilities of a cloud service consumer include managing the following security controls:

- Public Key Infrastructure (PKI)
- Security Development Life Cycle (SDLC)
- Web Application Firewall (WAF)
- Firewall
- Encryption

- Intrusion Prevention Systems
- Secure Web Gateway
- Application Security
- Virtual Private Network (VPN) and others

Resiliency and Automation Strategies

- Automation/Scripting
- Templates
- Master Image
- Non-Persistence
- Elasticity
- Scalability
- Distributive Allocation
- Redundancy
- Fault Tolerance
- High Availability
- RAID

Cloud Security Tools

Core CloudInspect

Core Security Technologies offer Core CloudInspect, a cloud security testing solution for Amazon Web Services (AWS). This tool benefits from Core Impact and Core Insight technologies to offer penetration testing as a service from Amazon Web Services for EC2 users.

CloudPassage Halo

CloudPassage Halo provides a broad range of security controls. It is a Focused Cloud Security Solution that prevents attacks and detects compromises. CloudPassage Halo operates under the ISO-27002 security standard and is audited annually against PCI Level 1 and SOC 2.

Chapter 20: Cryptography

Cryptography Concepts

Cryptography

Cryptography is a technique of encrypting clear text data into scrambled code. The encrypted data is then sent over a public or private network toward its destination to ensure confidentiality. This encrypted data, known as "Ciphertext", is decrypted at the destination for processing. Strong encryption keys are used to avoid key cracking. The objective of cryptography is not purely about confidentiality; it also concerns integrity, authentication, and non-repudiation.

Types of Cryptography

Symmetric Cryptography

The key that is symmetric in the field of cryptography, cryptography is the earliest and most extensively used cryptography technique. For data encryption and decryption, symmetric cyphers use the same secret key. AES and DES are the most extensively used symmetric cyphers.

Asymmetric Cryptography/Public Key Cryptography

Unlike Symmetric Ciphers, in Asymmetric Cryptography, two keys are used. Everyone publically knows one key, while the other key is kept secret and is used to encrypt data by the sender; hence, it is also called Public Key Cryptography. Each sender uses its secret key (also known as a Private Key) for encrypting its data before sending it. The receiver uses the respective sender's public key to decrypt the data. RSA, DSA, and the Diffie-Hellman Algorithm are popular examples of asymmetric ciphers. Asymmetric key cryptography delivers confidentiality, integrity, authenticity, and non-repudiation using public and private key concepts. The private key is only known by the owner itself, whereas the public key is issued by Public Key Infrastructure (PKI), where a trusted Certificate Authority (CA) certifies the ownership of key pairs.

Government Access to Keys (GAK)

Government Access to Keys (GAK) refers to agreements between government and software companies. All or necessary keys are delivered to a governmental organization, which keeps them securely and only uses them when a court issues a warrant.

Encryption Algorithms

- Ciphers
- Substitution
- Stream Cipher
- Block Cipher

Data Encryption Standard (DES)

Data Encryption Standard (DES) algorithm is a symmetric key algorithm used for encryption that is now considered insecure. However, successors such as Triple-DES and G-DES have replaced DES encryption. DES uses a 56-bit key size that is too small to protect data.

Advanced Encryption Standard (AES)

When DES becomes insecure and performing DES encryption three times (3-DES or Triple-DES) takes high computation and time, another encryption algorithm is needed that is more secure and effective. Rijndael issued a new algorithm in 2000-2001 known as Advanced Encryption Algorithm (AES). AES is also a private key symmetric algorithm, but it is stronger and faster than Triple-DES. AES can encrypt 128-bit data with 128/192/256-bit keys.

RC4, RC5, RC6 Algorithms

RC4 is an earlier encryption algorithm based on stream cypher that Ron Rivest created in 1987. SSL and WEP protocols both use RC4. RC4 creates a pseudorandom stream that is used to encrypt plain text using bit-wise exclusive-or encryption (similar to the Vernam cypher except for the generated pseudorandom bits).

RC5 is a symmetric key block cipher introduced in 1994. RC5 has variable block sizes (32, 64, or 128 bits) with a key size of 0 to 2040 bits and 0 to 255 rounds. It is suggested that RC5 is used with the 64-bit block size, 128-bit key, and 12 rounds. RC5 also consists of some modular additions and exclusive OR (XOR)s.

RC6 is also a symmetric key block cipher that is derived from RC5 with a block size of 128 bits with 128-,192-,256- and up to 2040-bit key support. RC6 is very similar to RC5 in structure, using data-dependent rotations, modular addition, and XOR operations. RC6 does use an extra multiplication operation not present in RC5 to make the rotation dependent.

RSA (Rivest Shamir Adleman)

Ron Rivest, Adi Shamir, and Leonard Adleman are the names of the algorithm's developers. The major objective of its use nowadays is authentication, and it is also known as Public Key Cryptography Standard (PKCS) #1. The key length can range from 512 to 2048 bits, with 1024 being the most common. One of the de facto encryption standards is RSA.

Message Digest (One-Way Hash) Functions

The Message Digest is a cryptographic hashing mechanism for ensuring a message's integrity. A communication channel can send a message and a message digest simultaneously or separately. To confirm that no changes have been done, a receiver recalculates the message's hash and compares it to the message digest.

Message Digest Function: MD5

The MD5 algorithm is from the message digest series. MD5 produces a 128-bit hash value used as a checksum to verify integrity. Hashing is the technique for ensuring integrity. The hash value is calculated by computing specific algorithms to verify data integrity to ensure it was not modified. Hash values play an important role in proving the integrity of documents and images and protocols to ensure the integrity of a transporting payload.

Secure Hashing Algorithm (SHA)

A Message Digest 5 (MD5) is a cryptographic hashing algorithm. The Secure Hashing Algorithm (SHA) is another more popular, secure, and widely used hashing algorithm is the Secure Hashing Algorithm (SHA). SHA-1 is a secure hashing algorithm producing a 160-bit hashing value compared to MD5, which produces a 128-bit value.

Secure Hash Algorithm 2 (SHA-2)

SHA2 has the option of varying a digest between 224 bits to 512 bits. SHA-2 is a group of different hashes, including SHA-256, SHA-384, and SHA 512. The stronger cryptographic algorithm will minimize the chances of compromise.

Hashed Message Authentication Code (HMAC)

HMAC uses the mechanism of hashing but adds the further feature of using a secret key in its operation. Both peers only know this secret key. Therefore, in this case, only parties with secret keys can calculate and verify the hash. By using HMAC, if there is an attacker eavesdropping, he/she will not be able to inject or modify the data and recalculate the correct hash because he/she will not know the correct key used by HMAC.

SSH (Secure Shell)

Secure Shell Protocol, commonly known in short as the SSH protocol, is a protocol used for secure remote connections. It is a secure alternative to insecure protocols such as Telnet, rlogin, and FTP. SSH is used for remote login and other protocols such as File Transfer Protocol (FTP) and Secure Copy Protocol (SCP). SFTP (SSH File Transfer Protocol) is popularly used for secure file transfer as it runs over SSH. SSH protocol functions over client-server architecture where the SSH client connects to the SSH server through a secure SSH channel over an insecure network.

Cryptography Tools

MD5 Hash Calculators

Several MD5 calculating tools are available that can directly calculate the hash value of text and offers to upload the desired file. Some of the most popular tools are:

1. HashCalc
2. MD5 Calculator
3. HashMyFiles

Hash Calculators for Mobile:

Hash calculating tools for mobile phones are:

- MD5 Hash Calculator
- Hash Droid
- Hash Calculator

Cryptography Tools

There are several tools available for encrypting files, such as the Advanced Encryption Package and BCTextEncoder. Similarly, some mobile cryptography applications are Secret Space Encryptor, CryptoSymm, and Cipher Sender.

Public Key Infrastructure (PKI)

Public Key Infrastructure

The policies, procedures, technology, software, and personnel necessary to create, administer, and revoke digital certificates are referred to as PKI. A Public Key Infrastructure (PKI) enables safe communication, data exchange, and money exchange between internet users and other public networks. A certificate authority provides public and private cryptographic key pairs for this purpose.

Public and Private Key Pair

In the encryption/decryption process, the Public and Private Key Pair operate together as a team. Everyone has access to the public key, while the private key is kept private. Nobody has access to a device's private key. We use the public key of a node to encrypt data transmitted to it. Similarly, the data is decrypted using the private key. In the opposite case, this is also true. When a node encrypts data using its private key, it uses its public key to decrypt it.

Certificate Authorities (CA)

A Certificate Authority (CA) is a machine or organization that creates and distributes digital certificates. The digital certificate contains information such as an IP address, a fully qualified domain name, and the public key of a specific device. The CA also gives the digital certificate a serial number and signs it with its digital signature.

- Root Certificate
- Identity Certificate
- Signed Certificate vs. Self-signed Certificate

Email Encryption

Digital Signature

A Digital Signature is a technique to evaluate the authenticity of digital documents as the signature authenticates the authenticity of a document. A digital signature confirms the author of the document, date, and time of signing and authenticates the content of the message.

There are two categories of digital signature:

1. Direct Digital Signature
2. Arbitrated Digital Signature

SSL (Secure Sockets Layer)

SSH stands for Secure Shell Protocol and is a protocol for creating secure remote connections. It is a secure alternative to unsecured protocols such as Telnet, rlogin, and FTP. In addition to remote login, SSH is utilized with additional protocols such as File Transfer Protocol (FTP) and Secure Copy Protocol (SCP). SFTP (SSH File Transmission Protocol) is frequently used for secure file transfer because it uses SSH. The SSH protocol uses a client-server architecture, with the SSH client communicating with the SSH server via a secure SSH channel over an unsecure network.

Pretty Good Privacy (PGP)

In RFC 4880, the Internet Engineering Task Force (IETFOpenPGP)'s Working Group defines it as a Proposed Standard. OpenPGP is derived from Phil Zimmermann's PGP software. OpenPGP's major goal is to provide end-to-end encryption for email communication and message encryption and decryption, a password manager, data compression, and digital signing.

Disk Encryption

Disk Encryption refers to the encryption of a disk to secure files and directories by converting the data into an encrypted format. Disk encryption encrypts every bit on the disk to prevent unauthorized access to data storage. There are several disk encryption tools available to secure disk volume, for example:

- Symantec Drive Encryption
- GiliSoft Full Disk Encryption

Cryptography Attacks

The goal of a cryptography attack is to retrieve an encryption key. An attacker can decrypt all messages once he or she knows the encryption key. Cryptographic attacks are not resistant enough to weak encryption techniques. Cryptanalysis is the process of identifying flaws in a code, encryption technique, or key management scheme. It can be used to either strengthen

or decrypt a cryptographic technique. Cryptography attacks include the following:
- Known Plaintext Attack
- Ciphertext-only Attack
- Chosen Plaintext Attack
- Chosen Ciphertext Attack
- Adaptive Chosen Ciphertext Attack
- Adaptive Chosen Plaintext Attack
- Rubber Hose Attack
- Collision
- Code Breaking Methodologies

Printed in Great Britain
by Amazon